The Imperial Archive

THE IMPERIAL ARCHIVE

Knowledge and the Fantasy of Empire

◆

THOMAS RICHARDS

London · New York

First published by Verso 1993
© Verso 1993
All rights reserved

Verso
UK: 6 Meard Street, London W1V 3HR
USA: 29 West 35th Street, New York, NY 10001–2291

Verso is the imprint of New Left Books

ISBN 978-0-86091-605-5

British Library Cataloguing in Publication Data
A catalogue record for this book is available from the British Library

Library of Congress Cataloging–in–Publication Data
A catalogue record for this book is available from the Library of Congress

Typeset by York House Typographic Ltd, London
Printed and bound in Great Britain by
Biddles Ltd, Guildford and King's Lynn

For Laura Hubber

CONTENTS

ACKNOWLEDGEMENTS

Thanks to Maggy Aston, Steve Austad, Walter Jackson Bate, Karsten Bondy, Peter Codella, Debbie Cohen, Jenny Davidson, Lydia Fillingham, Barbara Freeman, Steve Goldsmith, Gary Harrison, Amy Hotch, Jeanette Hubber, Veronika Kiklevich, Herbie Lindenberger, Lucy Morton, my parents Thomas and Joan Richards, Robert Richards, Richard Rogers, Priscilla Sneff, Marta Reid Stewart, Jeffrey Stewart, Will Stone, Theo Theoharis and Bill Todd. I am grateful for the support of the National Humanities Center, where I wrote the final draft of this book, and for a Hyder Rollins grant from the English Department at Harvard University. Thanks too to my editor at Verso, Malcolm Imrie, and to Laura Hubber. This book is for Laura.

INTRODUCTION

An empire is partly a fiction. No nation can close its hand around the world; the reach of any nation's empire always exceeds its final grasp. An empire is by definition and default a nation in overreach, one nation that has gone too far, a nation that has taken over too many countries too far away from home to control them effectively. All the great historical empires, ancient and modern, have had to come to terms with the problems of control at a distance. Empires may have armies and navies, but they also have messengers, or systems for conveying messages. The distance involved in conquest makes travel hard and knowledge of far-flung places difficult, as most of the old stories told about empires testify. In the *Odyssey* Penelope has no idea what Ulysses has been up to until he returns to tell his story. After the Battle of Marathon the messenger dies. Prospero goes off to an island and has to use magic to know what is going on around him. The ocean swallows up the argosies in *The Merchant of Venice*. Robinson Crusoe gets stuck on an island. The list goes on and on, at least until the middle of the nineteenth century, when – thanks to a new set of ideas about the nature of long-distance control, ideas largely scientific in origin, borrowed from the new disciplines of geography, biology and thermodynamics – people in Britain began to think differently about what it meant to hold on to an empire. The narratives of the late nineteenth century are full of fantasies about an empire united not by force but by information.

The study of some of these narratives is the subject of this book. From the beginning of the new imperialism in the 1860s, the British viewed their empire as an immense administrative challenge. Nobody in Britain ever thought seriously about occupying most of the red blotches on the world map of empire. The idea was to dominate them informally, using a combination of military might, economic muscle, and political pull. Politics usually came in a distant third, and most of the bright red countries on the imperial map, the newly annexed ones, had behind them a history of crazy military forays and bizarre get-rich-quick schemes. The scramble for Africa was just that, and a good number of the countries added to the Empire in the 1880s and 1890s had, in comparison with India or Australia, very little contact of any kind with Britain. 'Belonging' to the British Empire was thus very often a fictive affiliation. When Cecil Rhodes said, 'I would annex the stars if I could,' he wasn't just bragging. The imperialists were planting flags on soil most people in Britain considered as remote as the moon. Even when they were lost, Victorian explorers often claimed the territory around them for the crown. Those in the Scott Expedition had no idea where they were when they snapped a picture of themselves standing at what they took to be the South Pole. The British presence in India was really a series of ghettos, and the one time the British fought a war to retain a measure of control over South Africa, they very nearly lost.

I have written the four essays in *The Imperial Archive* to try to understand what it means to think the fictive thought of imperial control. Inside its borders a nation really can exert a lot of effective control. Most of the procedures of control Michel Foucault spent his life studying are the internal prerogatives of the single nation-state. Prisons, schools, armies are national institutions. Few nations bother to imprison people for crimes committed elsewhere, and when they do, as the recent case of Panama's Mañuel Noriega shows, it is highly controversial. When the Ayatollah Khomeini called for Salman Rushdie's head, it stunned everyone because he was trying to push one nation's death penalty over the line of the nation. During the Vietnam War all a resister had to do to evade the draft was skip across the border to Canada. Most nations have little say in what goes on outside their borders, as the history of the United Nations shows (often difficult to enact and enforce, international law often verges on a loose structure of fictions). Outside the unit of the nation, quick intervention or temporary occupation are not the exception but the rule. But though the control exerted by one nation over another doesn't last long and is constantly breaking apart, hardly anyone wants to admit this. The usual recourse here is to make national identity look like the template for imperial identity, to press fungible national symbols like the coat of arms or the escutcheon of Queen Victoria into imperial service. The symbolism of the British Empire was built on an extended foundation of national symbols. Proclaiming Victoria 'Empress of India' was a step in this direction. More concrete was the steady extension into the colonial world of domestic institutions like the British Museum. Throughout the nineteenth century the British liked to talk about their empire as if it were a sort of extended nation, and in a few isolated countries it was. Generally it was not. But seeing it that way, through the distorting lens of the nation, lent the Empire the sense of symbolic unity that it so often lacked in practice.

I have found that historians have tended to confer a lot more unity on the British Empire than is justified. Most people during the nineteenth century were aware that their empire was something of a collective improvisation. In the heyday of the Empire the Foreign Office was small and overworked. A lot was going on, so much that the Foreign Office, which had been set up to deal with intra-European affairs, simply was not able to keep up with it all. No one office ever administered the British Empire; lacking any standing imperial bureaucracy, it was overseen by a sort of extended civil service recruited from Britain's dominant classes. The work of the Foreign Office was often done by any educated person, however unqualified, working in whatever department, stationed wherever, who felt he had to do it simply because he happened to be British. These people were painfully aware of the gaps in their knowledge and did their best to fill them in. The filler they liked best was information. From all over the globe the British collected information about the countries they were adding to their map. They surveyed and they mapped. They took censuses, produced statistics. They made vast lists of birds. Then they shoved the data they had collected into a shifting series of classifications. In fact they often could do little other than collect and collate information, for any exact civil control, of the kind possible in England, was out of the question. The Empire was too far away, and the bureaucrats of Empire had to be content to shuffle papers.

This paper shuffling, however, proved to have great influence. It required keeping track, and keeping track of keeping track. It required some kind of archive for it all. Unquestionably the British

Empire was more productive of knowledge than any previous empire in history. The administrative core of the Empire was built around knowledge-producing institutions like the British Museum, the Royal Geographical Society, the India Survey, and the universities (many of the figures of imperial myth, from T.E. Lawrence to Indiana Jones, started out in some institution of higher learning). The ideology of mid-Victorian positivism had also led most people into believing that the best and most certain kind of knowledge was the fact. The fact was many things to many people, but generally it was thought of as raw knowledge, knowledge awaiting ordering. The various civil bureaucracies sharing the administration of Empire were desperate for these manageable pieces of knowledge. They were light and movable. They pared the Empire down to file-cabinet size. The British may not have created the longest-lived empire in history, but it was certainly one of the most data-intensive. The civil servants of Empire pulled together so much information and wrote so many books about their experiences that today we have only begun to scratch the surface of their archive. In a very real sense theirs was a paper empire: an empire built on a series of flimsy pretexts that were always becoming texts.

The truth, of course, is that it was much easier to unify an archive composed of texts than to unify an empire made of territory, and that is what they did – or at least tried to do, for most of the time they were unable to unify the knowledge they were collecting. It fell apart: ran off in many different directions like the hedgehogs in Alice's game of croquet, so much so that, in the chapters that follow, I question whether the data they collected can even be called 'knowledge.' Most Victorian epistemologies presupposed a superintending unity of knowledge. A comprehensive knowledge of the world was for most of the century the explicit goal of all forms of learning. People began the nineteenth century believing that all the knowledge in the world fell into a great standing order, a category of categories, but, after dozens of Casaubons had failed to make sense of thousands of facts squeezed into library catalogues, biological taxonomies, and philological treatises, they ended it by believing that the order of things was easier said than done. By 1900 not even the librarians at the British Museum seriously believed they would be able to chip away at this backlog of knowledge. The great monument to Victorian knowledge, the Oxford English Dictionary, wasn't completed until the late 1920s, by which time the first volumes in the series were already fifty years out of date. The intention had been to deal with old words, but there were too many new words and too many foreign words. The practical experience of trying to order all the incoming knowledge from the Empire had forced them to reconsider whether knowledge could ever in fact be unified. These people had found themselves in the midst of the first knowledge explosion. If today we call this the 'information explosion,' it was because by the century's end many people had stopped using the word 'knowledge,' which always had something about it of a prospective unity emerging, and started using the word 'information,' with its contemporary overtones of scattered disjunct fragments of fact.

This book, however, is not a history of the information explosion. I began writing it when I started to wonder why the literature of the late nineteenth century was so obsessed with the control of knowledge. Notice that I say 'the control of knowledge' rather than 'the control of empire.' For never has the alliance between knowledge and power been more clearly presented than in turn-of-the-century fiction. The four chapters of this book give readings of works by Kipling, Stoker, Wells, and Childers, in which knowledge acts as much more than a convenient surrogate for power. In *Kim* (1901), *Dracula* (1897), *Tono-Bungay* (1909) and *The Riddle of the Sands* (1903), the pursuit of knowledge is the vanguard, not the rearguard, of the pursuit of power. In *Kim*, the India Survey, a geographical bureau, defeats a Russian plot to extend influence in the Indian subcontinent. In *Dracula*, a monster is defeated by mastery of the means of information. *Tono-Bungay* ends with a vision of science in the service of the state, and *The Riddle of the Sands* with an essay appended by Childers calling for the mobilization of all the knowledge in Britain. Each of the novels equates knowledge with national security. Each sees a British mastery of the means of knowledge as overpowering threats to empire. And each goes so far as to see knowledge itself not as the supplement of power but as its replacement in the colonial world. In these novels knowledge defeats power every time. And no wonder: the nineteenth century had seen time collapsed and space contracted as never before. Technologies like the railway, the steamship, the telegraph and the telephone made it possible for people to imagine knowing things not sequentially but

simultaneously. The great Victorian projects of knowledge all had at
their center a dream of knowledge driven into the present. The new
disciplines of geography, biology, and thermodynamics all took as
their imperium the world as a whole, and worked out paradigms of
knowledge which seemed to solve the problem of imperial control at
a distance. In geography the map masters distance, in geology the
fossil record masters time, in thermodynamics the experiment masters movement. The fiction I will be examining is full of the rhetoric
of the imperial sciences and plays it out in plots in which recording
the Empire, making a vast record of it using the new knowledges,
becomes tantamount to controlling it. These novels and others like
them, which I will be looking at in some detail, go so far as to create
a myth of a unified archive, an imperial archive holding together the
vast and various parts of the Empire.

This archive was neither a library nor a museum, though imperial
fiction is full of little British libraries and museums scattered all over
the globe. Rather the imperial archive was a fantasy of knowledge
collected and united in the service of state and Empire. Though a
literary fantasy, it was shared widely and actually had an impact on
policy-making. Its impact can be quickly summed up by the way in
which the word 'classification' changed its meaning in the late
nineteenth century. At mid-century it meant ordering information in
taxonomies; by century's end 'classified' had come to mean knowledge placed under the special jurisdiction of the state. In the fantasy
of the imperial archive, the state actually succeeds in superintending
all knowledge, particularly the great reams of knowledge coming in
from all parts of the Empire. The myth of imperial archive brought
together in fantasy what was breaking apart in fact, and it did so by
conjoining two different conceptions of knowledge that may at first
seem contradictory. These are the ideas of a knowledge at once
positive and *comprehensive*. The familiar Victorian project of positive knowledge divided the world into little pieces of fact. A fact was
a piece of knowledge asserted as certain, and positive knowledge
was considered by both Mill and Comte to be the sum of objectively
verifiable facts. The problem here of course was that facts almost
never added up to anything. They were snippets of knowledge, tiny
particularized units responsible for our current idea of information.
It took a leap of faith to believe that facts would someday add up to
any palpable sum of knowledge, and that faith often took the form

of an allied belief in comprehensive knowledge. Comprehensive knowledge was the sense that knowledge was singular and not plural, complete and not partial, global and not local, that all knowledges would ultimately turn out to be concordant in one great system of knowledge. This system-building impulse was the imperial archive's great inheritance from a philosophical tradition that posited a universal and essential form of knowledge, the tradition of Leibnitz and Kant and von Humboldt, but it also took much the same ideas from a source nearer to hand, English Romanticism. Indeed it turned out that Romanticism contributed a great deal to imagining the Empire as a concordant whole. The impulse toward the universal in Shelley, the project of a complete knowledge of the world in Coleridge, the ability of Blake's visions to span the globe, the sense of a fully surveyed landscape in Wordsworth: these differing but exhaustive projects were carried forward in the literature of Empire examined here. Though a domestic school of poetry, English Romanticism was imperial in the scope of its often-failed ambitions. In the Victorian period, Romanticism persists not only as a source of imagery for empire (the Romantic poets discovered and refined the imagery of orientalism, providing staples for travel writers and novelists alike), but as the basic animating project of the imperial archive, namely, the organization of all knowledges into a coherent imperial whole. The Victorian contribution was simply to reformulate this project as explicitly imperial and redeploy the stock imagery of Romanticism to serve the end and aims of Empire. The legacy of Romanticism was the residual conviction most Victorians shared that all knowledge, despite its modular character, should and would be united. Knowledge was expanding rapidly, but so were the means to contain it. The peculiarly Victorian confidence that knowledge could be controlled and controlling, that knowledge could be exploding and yet be harnessed as the ultimate form of power, issued from this felt merger of the Victorian project of positive knowledge with the Romantic project of comprehensive knowledge. The merger of these two projects made possible the fantasy of an imperial archive in which the control of Empire hinges on a British monopoly over knowledge.

This supplanting of power by the force of knowledge is one of the hallmarks of the twentieth century. Much of what I talk about in

The Imperial Archive is in effect a working back from our own world, a world in which armies fund universities, corporations run laboratories, banks sponsor the arts. Power now draws its breath from knowledge, and knowledge exhales in an iron lung. Today we routinely assume that no power can possible exist without its underlay of documents, memoranda, licenses, and files. Obvious as it may now seem, this assumption was new in the nineteenth century, when a great variety of novelists saw it being worked out in front of their eyes. If this book is mostly a work of literary criticism, it is because literature got to the subject first. Fifty years before Norbert Wiener coined the word 'cybernetics,' British writers were examining in detail the role information played in legitimating the British Empire. Two of my chapters end with discussion of Thomas Pynchon's *Gravity's Rainbow* (1973), and I have often returned to this American work of fiction because it is set in the London of 1944 and gives a picture of the chilling presence of power among the mandarins of knowledge. Pynchon's novel is poised between two empires. In it the British decant what they have learned into an intelligence network run by Americans, and the Americans learn their lesson well. The British Empire had colonies. Today's American Empire thinks not about occupying land but about watching it, and calls its colonies satellites.

This is a book, then, about the British Empire not as it was but as it was imagined to have been. This emphasis on the fantasy of empire accounts for the primary position a series of literary readings occupies in this book. It also accounts for the fact that not all of the texts discussed deal with the Empire directly. Rather than trying to survey the entire literature of the British Empire, I have searched for the most distinctive features of the British imperial imagination. Slavery, conquest, violence, deportation, ethnocide: these are features of most empires, and though they are the focus of the work of a great imperial novelist, Joseph Conrad, they tend to play a markedly marginal role in most imperial fiction. Imperial fiction is far more frequently the site of fantasy rather than realism. Many of the typical features of this imperial fantasy have already been located and enumerated. Our understanding of the fantasies of empire, of the processes by which fantasy repels and replaces history, has been much enhanced by many recent studies probing the specific discourses and genres of empire (Edward Said on orientalism and

Patrick Brantlinger on imperial gothic are exemplary here). This book seeks to add the relation between information and imperialism to this list. The fantasy of the imperial archive was a distinctive product of the late nineteenth century, as compelling in its way as the discourse of orientalism or the genre of imperial gothic. The obsession with gathering and ordering information has so far passed unremarked in imperial fiction. This book works to restore a large and missing dimension to our understanding of the imperial imagination as it applied itself to perceiving the colonial world in the nineteenth and twentieth centuries. Though I have confined myself to a few representative examples, the underlying concern with the problems of knowledge and information can be found everywhere in imperial fiction. Understanding the fantasy of knowledge elevated to global power takes us a long way toward understanding the lure, and finally the persistence, of the much larger fantasy of empire itself.

ONE

ARCHIVE AND UTOPIA

This chapter is about the opening and closing of a utopian space of comprehensive knowledge in the nineteenth and early twentieth centuries. It locates a geopolitical domain in which nineteenth-century British geographers situated the nerve center of all possible knowledge, the library of all libraries and the museum of all museums. It traverses an interval of time, between 1870 and 1940, during which institutions like the British Museum could not keep up with all the knowledge they were amassing, a period in history when the task of collecting and classifying knowledge increasingly fell to civil servants operating under state supervision. Victorian England charged a variety of state facilities with the special task of maintaining the possibility of comprehensive knowledge. This operational field of projected total knowledge was the archive. The archive was not a building, nor even a collection of texts, but the collectively imagined junction of all that was known or knowable, a fantastic representation of an epistemological master pattern, a virtual focal point for the heterogeneous local knowledge of metropolis and empire. Though in theory, as Michel Foucault has written, 'the archive cannot be described in its totality,' in nineteenth-century British practice the archive was often figured as a fixed place, as a discrete institution, even as a single person.[1] The ordering of the world and its knowledges into a unified field was located explicitly in the register of representation, where, most successfully of all, the archive often took the imagined form of a utopian state.

In the late nineteenth and early twentieth centuries, the prevalent model for the archival confinement of total knowledge under the purview of the state was Tibet, an imagined community that united archival institutions and persons in one hieratic archive-state. In

geography was state policy). Colonel Thomas Holdich, Superinten-
dent of Frontier Surveys in India from 1892 to 1898, knew very well
that 'geographical surveys are functions of both civil and military
operations.' The survey used base measurements, geodetic triangu-
lation, telegraph determination, route surveying, tacheometry,
phototopography, and ferrotype reproduction to generate a map of
India in the detailed scale of one inch to a mile. The survey
proceeded square mile by square mile, gradually taking cadastral
possession of the entire country, stopping just at its borders. Under
Captain Thomas Montgomerie, a Royal Engineers officer who later
cast a long shadow over Kipling's *Kim*, Tibetan space underwent a
similar process of semioticization. The smooth and undifferentiated
space of the old blank map became the striated and specialized space
peculiar to the discipline of geography. In modified form the techniques of geography were deployed to generate an archival representation of Tibet: the project's success established it as a prototype for
the ways in which the archival technology of the exact sciences could
shape perceptions of time and space within a given sector. Just as
importantly, the completed map of Tibet became a working model
for the ways in which the production of knowledge could act as the
vanguard of the state in situations where, as Holdich put it 'a
country lies open to exploration, not actively hostile, but yet
unsettled and averse to strangers.'[4]

Like the American project that constructed the first cyclotron and
housed a weapons research laboratory in the basement of an institution of higher learning, the Tibetan project was conducted under the
joint auspices of the India Survey and the British Museum. This
conjunction was productive and influential. Long before the Secret
Service played a prominent role in retrieving and storing information for the Empire, an unofficial network of Victorian learned
societies acted as the central clearing-house for British imperial
intelligence about Tibet.[5] The Victorian state had long maintained
an informal but searching interest in those who sought to develop
new technologies for extending control over knowledge, but in the
political imagination of late-Victorian Britain, the principal model
for imagining this interface between knowledge and the state was
the archive. In imperial mythology the archive was less a specific
institution than an entire epistemological complex for representing a comprehensive knowledge within the domain of Empire.

Pre-eminent among the knowledge-producing institutions of Empire, the British Museum was charged with the collection of classified knowledge, both ordered knowledge and, increasingly, secret knowledge, but a variety of other institutions like the Royal Geographical Society, the Royal Society, and the Royal Asiatic Society also formed part of what was widely imagined as an imperial archive. In late-Victorian literature this archive took the form not of a specific institution but of an ideological construction for projecting the epistemological extension of Britain into and beyond its empire. Late-Victorian writers liked to conceive of a complex of British archives extending its tentacles informally all over the Empire, and they produced a variety of representations that showed the formal security apparatus of the late-Victorian state (the Secret Service, the Foreign Office) recruiting its personnel and deriving its technologies of surveillance from the geographical, demographic, and ethnographic practices devised by the various learned societies to produce and classify comprehensive knowledge about the Empire. Many historians have long considered the nineteenth-century museum a crashing failure as an institution – as Edward Miller has shown, the British Museum was underfunded by Parliament and overburdened with data for most of the nineteenth century – but what the imperial archive signally succeeded in doing was to establish itself at the center of Victorian and early-twentieth-century representation. Widely deplored at home by its administrators as a bottomless pit of knowledge, it was widely celebrated in imperial popular culture as the key to the mythologies of Victorian life.

The place of the British Museum in late-Victorian culture provides an exemplary instance of the confluence of the aesthetic and political spheres of representation. In a very general way the capillaries of an institution like the British Museum traversed the British Empire, and as a political institution the museum tended to intervene forcefully in the Empire (where cultural treasures often needed to be taken by force). Far from having its activities restricted to the reading room of Antonio Panizzi's iron library, where the circulation desk dispensed books at the library's hub, the reach of the museum extended across the globe. By 1867 nine of its ten departments carried on the bulk of their work outside the walls of the museum and, like many other Victorian societies, the museum sponsored knowledge-gathering expeditions in the colonial world.[6] But institutions like the India Survey operated locally, gathering local knowledge, codifying it, and translating it into the language of the state, which was increasingly the language of the archive. The India Survey equipped the Raj with a vast internal system of files, dossiers, censuses, statistics, maps, and memoranda.[7] It worked at the precise threshold where the classification of knowledge produced classified, or secret, knowledge. The India Survey also provides a clear example of the process by which an imagined epistemology could intervene to shape the political definition of actual territory. In the series of procedures that the state-organized survey devised to classify Tibet, the archive functioned both to imagine territory as representation and realize it as a social construction. What began as utopian fictions of knowledge, in other words, often ended as territory. This system of representational order – an order of social imagination so powerful that it could, in effect, construct social reality – was responsible for fashioning the modern idea of Tibet.

Despite its imagined central location in institutions such as the British Museum, the Victorian conception of the imperial archive had a remarkably modular structure.[8] The centralization of knowledge was widely portrayed as decentralized. In fact most official Victorian archivists were amateurs – like T.E. Lawrence, who began by joining the 1909 British Museum expedition to Jerablus on the Upper Euphrates to search for the site of Hittite Carchemish and then drifted into government service – and they improvised a great number of unconventional methods to produce conventional knowledge for the domestic archive. At home the officials associated with the British Museum placed knowledge in provisional classifications that were the object of unending dispute in Parliament and among the intelligentsia. Examined closely, the grand narrative of the nineteenth-century archive fragments into smaller narratives of interdepartmental disputation and finally into autonomous practices – such as the image of the British Museum 'basement,' a peripheral zone of lost or forgotten knowledge buried deep within the catacombs of the London archive.[9] Among the officialdom of empire, too, tactics governed strategy; in the field, as Clausewitz had written in *On War* (1831), 'everything is more mobile, and psychological forces, individual differences, and chance play a more influential part.'[10] The same can be said for the frontiers of the

British Empire, a shifting series of points in a heterogeneous space capable of constant redefinition. There the work of the archive was an ongoing labor in the face of almost insuperable obstacles. To these imperial hierophants the Victorian archive was no more than a vast assemblage for circulating knowledge between the various specialized cordons of empire; mired in detail, they could see no further than can the preoccupied bureaucrats in Kipling's *Plain Tales from the Hills* (1890). Seen from the perspective of our own information society, however, the Victorian archive appears as a prototype for a global system of domination through circulation, an apparatus for controlling territory by producing, distributing, and consuming information about it. Formerly a blank space on the map, Tibet was about to become one of the most overcoded spaces in the British Empire.

The mapping of Tibet required the imposition of a new kind of grid. The India Survey possessed powers that were, at least technically speaking, uniform and seamless. Bit by bit it had divided India into a cellular network of quadrants. The Tibetan government, however, had refused to allow the kind of generalized access this procedure required. The British had not originally intended to classify the Tibetan project as secret knowledge; like the architects of the German autobahn in the 1930s or the American interstate road system in the 1950s, they wanted to lay out a civil network that could serve as a military artery at an unspecified later date. The Tibetans' refusal transformed an ordinary expedition for classifying geographical knowledge into a classified project for surveying alien terrain. The Tibetan project thus became a behind-the-lines operation in which the 'lines' in question were not those of an enemy (Britain was not at war with Tibet) but rather lines on a map. The obvious difficulty of mapping a country without entering it called for new forms of geographical technology. To rephrase Clausewitz's famous dictum, if nineteenth-century geography was the continuation of politics by other means, the political situation in Tibet would now require the continuation of geography by other means.

The genius of the Tibetan project was that it assembled a whole museum of ancient technologies to survey Himalayan space. Barred from entering Tibet because of 'political complication,' Captain Montgomerie noticed that 'natives of India passed freely backwards and forwards between Ladak [in northeast India] and Yarkund [in central Tibet].'[11] Montgomerie decided to disguise his surveyors as monks. In 1862 he trained the first of a series of Hindu pundits in the uses of basic instrumentation – compass, sextant, and thermometer. Bearings or azimuths were taken with a compass, latitudes with the sextant, altitudes by recording the temperature at which water boiled. Like the devices that Ian Fleming's 'Q' designs for James Bond, the instruments had been miniaturized by the Survey of India workshops. Robes were lined with secret pockets, compasses were fitted inside the top knobs of spiked pilgrims' staffs (which also served as makeshift tripods), thermometers were concealed in hollowed-out staves, extra mercury (used for setting an artificial horizon while taking sextant readings) was sealed in a cowrie shell and poured into a pilgrim's bowl wherever needed, sextants were squirreled away in false-bottomed chests. In seconds the line of monks could begin producing 'readings,' in a sense of the word that first appeared in the mid nineteenth century: no longer the interpretation of texts but the indication of graduated instruments.[12]

Unlike James Bond, who foils his adversaries with the help of various high-tech devices, Montgomerie became one of the first imperialists to adapt local practices to produce knowledge of a locale. With much effort he trained his recruits to walk up, down, or on the level at a set pace. He also taught them to count the number of paces they took in a day, and to keep count by using a Buddhist rosary. A rosary did not have to be hidden, but to simplify matters Montgomerie had special rosaries built with 100 rather than the customary 108 beads so that they could be used as decimal abacuses. The average monk stride turned out to be 33 inches. Every hundredth pace a monk slipped a bead. Every complete circuit of the rosary meant ten thousand paces, or five miles. Montgomerie's first map merely showed a single line zigzagging across empty space, but it also constructed a new political regime of knowledge, able, as he reported to his superiors, to 'give us an intelligible idea as to the whole of Eastern Turkistan.'[13] For not only did Montgomerie's monastic technology integrate topological surveillance into the rhythm of everyday Tibetan life (thus making it imperceptible), but it also introduced a paradigm of surveillance as a migratory phenomenon (thus rendering obsolete the fixed fortifications of blockhouse, conning tower, escarpment and frontier). At one and the same time the Tibetan project combined an ancient form of measuring extended space using body-based units of measure (as with the span and the fathom), a medieval form of clocking time by dividing the day into units of prayer (as called for by St Benedict's *Rule*), and a modern form for vehicular surveillance by projectile. In an uncanny way Montgomerie's project presents us with a prescient vision of outmoded technologies performing the most advanced functions of surveillance, construction, and representation. It shows a world in which old technology keeps pace with new, obsolescence produces innovation, the past enables the future. The point here is that advanced technologies of power do not supersede older forms, like motorways replacing passenger trains; rather they are coextensive with them. Montgomerie's project used subsidiary technologies to supplement and finally to surpass the most advanced techniques available to him. The necessity of secrecy drove him to reconstruct the past, placing it in a kind of working museum at the service of the state. In *Kim* the museum curator notices 'the mixture of old-world piety and modern progress that is the note of India today.'[14] In Franz Kafka's *The Castle* (1926), another text in which the main character is a land surveyor, an advanced bureaucracy inhabits a medieval town. Montgomerie, too, reached into the past and resurrected a technological lineage of methods for constructing time and projecting space. Though he clearly viewed himself not as a spy but as a surveyor, his surveying provided the Raj with intelligence of a potential rather than an actual kind (when Britain finally invaded Tibet in 1903–4, the soldiers carried corrected versions of the maps Montgomerie had generated). Like many Victorian learned societies that developed and refined advanced philosophical techniques for deciphering dead languages, his project – a data pilgrimage utilizing a rapid deployment force of monks – appropriated and reorganized older systems of transfer, transit, and transmission. The result was a combined regression and progression of basic technology oriented toward what can be termed a *state nomadology*.

The idea of 'nomadology' has been formulated by Gilles Deleuze and Felix Guattari in *A Thousand Plateaus* (1980) to grasp the capacities and limits of the state in the nineteenth and twentieth centuries. In the figure of the 'nomad,' they see embodied all the fugitive forces that European states since the early modern period have sought to contain and destroy. The nomadic sums up everything that has remained counter to the state, including knowledges that resist bureaucratic codification (think of orally transmitted Theravadin texts), peoples that defy national concentration (think of Jews, gypsies, indigenous tribes), armies that evade defeat (think of Boer guerrillas in 1900), entire societies that inhibit the formation of power centers (think of the Guarani Indians studied by Pierre Clastres). In a sense nomadology can best be understood as an extended gloss to a pair of Kafka stories, 'The Great Wall' and 'An Old Manuscript.' In the first an ancient Chinese engineer wonders why the Great Wall has been built according to a system of piecemeal construction, with bits going up here and there, when 'not only can such a wall not protect, but what there is of it is in perpetual danger.' In the second there has been a collective failure of nerve as the functionaries of the Chinese state await destruction at the hands of nomads who have penetrated a series of blockades and now threaten not only the surviving polity but language itself: 'Speech with the nomads is impossible. They do not know our language, indeed they hardly have a language of their own.'[15] Together these stories advance a proleptic vision in which state policies of population containment have failed, and the state is moving toward fragmentation. Their speakers are functionaries who desperately try to draw attention to the nomads before it is too late. Like the Kipling of 'Recessional' (1897), whom so many of his contemporaries found incomprehensible, they argue that the state must not only confront its extraterritorials but must territorialize them in such a way that the state can begin to employ nomadic powers that were once alien to it. The primitive must become the ultramodern.

However accurate the final map may have been, however, the nomadic registration of Tibetan space did not and could not achieve full realization for the simple reason that it had been performed by indigenous nomadic labor. In his 1906 *Tibet the Mysterious*, Colonel Holdich casts doubt on the self-sufficient intelligibility of the territorial representations produced by members of a different race: 'It is often a little difficult to obtain a really graphic and intelligible account of the country explored from the native surveyors who explore it. They become so engrossed with the details of their work that they forget to use their eyes and make those general observations on the people and the scenery about them which is a most important objective of their journeyings.'[16] Holdich makes it clear that geography was a necessary but not sufficient tool for realizing territory. It must always be accompanied by the imperatives of state ethnography, which territorialize a domain not only by mapping it but by producing all manner of 'thick' description about it. The survey is only one form of ethnographic surveillance, and it tends to produce a homogeneous, geometric space rather than an accidental heterogeneous space. Like Clausewitz, who also stresses the secondary role of geometry in strategy and tactics, Holdich takes as his ideal a map that is completely coextensive with the territory it purports to represent.

Such a map can only be produced by Western agency. In *Erewhon* (1872) Samuel Butler relates a myth of the mountain-bound Erewhonians (who, like the Tibetans, live on a high plateau) that shows how they have adjusted themselves to the necessarily partial mapping of the territory they inhabit. It seems that the Erewhonians view existence as an unfolding map that they can never quite comprehend. 'They say,' Butler writes, 'that the future and the past are as a panorama upon two rollers; that which is on the roller of the future unwraps itself on to the roller of the present. . . . It is ever unwinding and being wound; we catch it in transition for a moment, and call it present.'[17] Unlike, say, the Tibetan explorer Sven Hedin, who took a series of seven photographs of a mountainscape and pieced them together to reconstruct an intelligible panorama, the inhabitants Erewhon have little or no access to comprehensive knowledge. Not only must knowledge be selectively imported to them and carefully reassembled on the spot, dispensed through branch offices of the imperial archive or some institution like the one that James Hilton will later call 'Shangri-La,' but the technology of territorial self-representation must remain in extraterritorial hands. Only the British can represent themselves, and only an occidental philosopher like Josiah Royce can bring himself in 1899 to imagine 'a map of England' projecting, 'down to the minutest details, every contour and marking, natural and artificial, that occurs upon the surface of England.'[18] By extension, only those capable of this kind of imagined self-representation can represent others. The Tibetan project had operated at the outer limits of local knowledge. A more complete territorialization of Tibet would require a comprehensive centralization of the knowledge that Montgomerie's operatives had so painstakingly collected in piecemeal fashion. It would require the fashioning of a vast and mobile zone of knowledge under a specialized kind of nomadic supervision, under a Western personage capable of combining the functions of soldier, ambassador, surveyor, scholar, and spy. In nineteenth-century fiction the archival subject who worked to attain comprehensive knowledge tended to break down under the pressure of information; without exception the individual archive dies (Casaubon), despairs (Bouvard and Pecuchet), splits (Dr Jekyll and Mr Hyde), or sinks (Captain Nemo). The territorialization of Tibet would require, in other words, the figuration of a new subject, an archival superman who would not self-destruct – Kipling's Colonel Creighton, the imperial archive's man for all seasons.

II

Kim is a narrative of the high command, its reckonings, its representatives, its projects, and its projections. No action takes place within the novel that cannot be integrated into the orbit of contingent necessities sanctioned by the state. The novel performs a work of assimilation: it codifies the wanderings of the many nomadic forces it contains, allowing them extraordinary latitude even as it adjusts them to accord with the implied decrees of the high command. The actions of the novel form a series of picaresque incidents that are random and accidental in name only, because, no matter how far they may seem to veer from the presence of a plan, they always take place in exact accordance with the dictates of headquarters. Yet the structure for the transmission of commands remains elusive. In *Kim* the high command does not constitute a primary social bond; the novel is full of distinctive national identities and includes Tibetans, Sikhs, Moslems, Hindus, and members of almost every caste in northeast Indian society. Rather the state constitutes a kind of infra-individual implant detached from the active consciousness of its subjects, while remaining an activating part of them. It is when Kim acts most quintessentially as an Irishman, Mahbub Ali as a Muslim, the Lama as a Tibetan, that they most further state designs that they are scarcely aware of. In *Kim* the Secret Service has become differentialized and deterritorialized, a system of local knowledge capable of pure circulation and indefinite proliferation; the novel is the first sustained narrative of state nomadology.

Kipling was one of the few people in his generation to appreciate the importance of Montgomerie's mapping of Tibet, and in various ways he places it at the center of his novel. What *Kim* figures more clearly than any other Victorian text is a world in which colonization through ethnocide, deportation, and slavery (the operations of a modern and premodern world) has begun to give way to colonization through the mediated instrumentality of information (the operations of a postmodern world). The novel deals with the problem of semicolonization, the problem of administering vast areas of unoccupiable land. Though Kipling shifts the setting of his novel from Himalayan Tibet to Himalayan India, he tells a story in which British civil surveillance, faced with a territory so vast and diverse that it could not possibly be occupied or obliterated, has become a procedure without territory. The perceived amorphousness of India, like the perceived impenetrability of Himalayan Tibet, created conditions in which the fixed occupation of an armed body gave way to a disembodied occupation without center or position.[19] *Kim* is a novel in which all social time and space is potentially a site of civil defense, and the great secret at the heart of the novel is precisely a knowledge of the time and place in which a confrontation between the mobile forces of the superpowers, England and Russia, will (or, depending on circumstances, will not) take place. The pursuit of that knowledge, undertaken under a variety of guises, animates the novel's narrative and illustrates the logistics of late Victorian state nomadology.

Kipling structures his novel around a plot of recruitment, and the novel might be seen to prefigure the United States Army's 1980s advertising slogan, 'Be all you can be.' *Kim* is a *Bildungsroman* in the service of the state. Foreshadowing the modern model of certain South American countries, which recruit their officer corps from orphanages, Kim begins the novel as a nomad and an orphan who gradually matures into a ward of the state, whose every movement, utterance, and experience replicates intangible state designs. His movements may seem undirected, his utterances vatic, his experiences chance events, but in time they fall into place with all the precision of what Kipling calls 'the art and science of mensuration'(211). In this novel it always turns out that, so far as the state is concerned, there is no such thing as a nonconducting medium; everyone and everything, consciously or unconsciously, forms part of the state's internal lines of communication. Kim undergoes a series of discipleships – first with the Tibetan Teshoo Lama, then with the Muslim Mahbub Ali, then with Lurgan Sahib, and finally with the Hindu Hurree Babu – all of which fashion for him a very fluid yet specialized identity as a member of the Secret Service. Neither 'Musselman, Hindu, Jain, or Buddhist,' Kim aspires to completeness by aspiring to the complete self-effacement of a code name such as R17, C25–IB, E23, or M4. 'If only, like Babu, he could enjoy the dignity of a letter and a number – and a price upon his head!'(210). In the world of *Kim*, Oscar Wilde's hated cell number, C.3.3., would be considered an honorific. The conjunction of letter, number, and price betokens not the penal servitude of the prison colony but the civil servitude of the archival state apparatus known as the India Survey, the all-encompassing bureau charged by the Raj with the capture, channeling, and storage of classified information.

Throughout *Kim* the state does its best to foster an information economy of extraordinarily low viscosity. The novel takes place amidst a shifting field of populations in central and northeast India. Kipling returns again and again to the spectacle of migration, 'a stately corridor' along which it was possible to see 'all India spread out to left and right'(111). Here, as elsewhere in his fiction, Kipling is fascinated by the orders of movements (the bridge in *The Bridge Builders*, the embankment in *Puck of Pook's Hill*, the hunt in *The Jungle Books*).[20] In *Kim* much of this movement takes place slowly, 'as the Orientals understand speed'(190), and the reason that the India Survey selects Kim as one of its own is that he displays almost no resistance to the nomadic flow of the road. The boy literally goes with the flow. He longs to escape from the applied force of his St Xavier's education, and he is happiest when, to use Mahbub Ali's metaphor, he is given free reign to drift at large along the corridors of interstate transportation. Along the Grand Trunk Road the coagulant forces of the police – buffoons whom Kipling subjects to ridicule – are not the only representatives of the polis. Rather Kipling shifts the policing function from one of periodic blockage (at stations like toll booths) to a more nomadic form of highway surveillance. Unlike, say, the traveler Richard Burton, who posed as a wandering dervish to gain entrance to the Tomb of the Prophet at

Medina in 1853, Kim infiltrates a community by actually joining it.[21] He does not travel incognito. Like the anarchists in G.K. Chesterton's *The Man Who Was Thursday* (1908), who conceal their conspiracies by plotting them openly in a public restaurant, he travels with a Red Lama, one of those individuals whom Kipling calls 'not inconspicuous persons' (269). No mere master of disguises, Kim is a master of identities who undertakes to gather information by becoming a simulacrum of that which he seeks to gather. He is a novice in the original sense of the word – a member of a novitiate awaiting initiation into a social order. Under the guidance of his various national mentors, Kim adapts himself to the circumstances and customs at hand, moving with ease into a state of environmental equilibrium with the road, its inhabitants, its taboos, and its procedures. He operates exclusively by means of local protocols and customs.

The prophecy that fuels the plot provides a striking example of Kim's fidelity to local protocol and custom. Kim takes to the road because he follows a prophetic call, which typically involves both abandoning a land (to go in search of another, promised land) and forsaking an existing system of norms (to found another). In India prophecy was also a vehicular mode of speech, usually undertaken by religious migrants and members of various mendicant orders. From the outset Kipling situates Kim's development within the indigenous structure of prophecy, and the first third of the novel moves the boy's life into alignment with the exact words of a prophecy concerning him: born under a 'sign of war,' '900 *pukka* devils and a Colonel riding of a horse will look after you when you find the red Bull [on a green field]' (50). Of course the prophecy ultimately leads Kim into the migratory orbit not of the Lama's religious order but of a regiment, which Kipling takes care initially to depict as adept in the nomadic art of encampment. Though at first prophecy seems to be external to the administration of the Raj, it turns out that it forms a deregulated part of the state, a loosely constructed space where, if Clastres is right, it may well be possible to locate 'the beginning of the State in the [prophetic] Word.'[22] Certainly in *Kim* prophecy and state power go hand in hand: all the novel's prophecies concern channels of mass transportation and rapid communication (river, road, railway, and regiment). The most prophetic figure in the novel, Huneeta the magician, does her work under state ethnological observation, which results in a scholarly article that Hurree Babu hopes will gain him entry into the Royal Society. In pursuit of his river prophesy the Lama's rosary, like that of Montgomerie's pundits, 'clicked furiously as an abacus' (142). And after describing Kim as the 'instrument' for the fulfillment of the Lama's prophecy, Kipling depicts Kim's enlightenment as instrumentally calibrated when 'with an almost audible click he felt the wheels of his being lock up anew on the world without' (331). The prophetic mission, the search for individual knowledge, has become indistinguishable from the state mission, the search-and-gather mission for classified information, the search-and-rescue mission of E23 on the train to Delhi, and the search-and-destroy mission of the Russian expedition to Tibet.

The prophetic state mission does not, however, entail any sort of comprehensive prior knowledge of events. On a grand scale the novel's many prophecies may invest its narrative with an aura of inevitability, but on a local level they function very much like a statistical field of possibility. Kipling says again and again that 'there was no purpose in his wanderings' (127), that Kim has given himself up to 'the play of circumstances' (165). He neither gives nor receives orders, but instead is periodically released onto the Boltzmannian world of the road, where, as the Austrian statistician wrote in 1899, 'the movements of a body do not occur purely accidentally, going sometimes here, sometimes there, but . . . they are completely determined by the circumstances to which the body is subject.'[23] In other words, the play of circumstances to which Kim is subject – a play of locations, arrangements, and replacements – is itself subject to a master pattern of possibility and impossibility.[24] Like Kipling (and most other late Victorian imperialists), Ludwig Boltzmann believed in a sort of indeterminate determination, an uncertain certainty, a calculable end to be reached by incalculable means. Kim does not require special facilities to serve the state; as an official *bricoleur* he uses whatever means are at hand, and it always turns out that a world structured by the play of circumstances is the best of all possible worlds. In effect the novel culminates in a Boltzmannian case study of unorchestrated design:

Here were the emissaries of the dread Power of the North, very possibly as great in their own Land as Mahbub or Colonel Creighton, suddenly smitten helpless. . . . Tonight they lay out somewhere below him, chartless, foodless, tentless, gunless – except for Hurree Babu, guideless. And this collapse of their Great Game (Kim wondered who they might report to), this panicky bolt into the night, had come about through no craft of Hurree's or contrivance of Kim's, but simply, beautifully, and inevitably. (297)

Like his earlier capture of the *fakir* who lay in wait to assassinate Mahbub, or his rough-and-ready makeover to disguise the wounded agent on the train to Delhi, Kim depends on the improvisation of necessity, the incidence of conformity to plan. As if to underscore the felt internal logic of the incident, Hurree Babu ends the chapter by rehearsing the geometric proposition that 'you cannot occupy two places in space simultaneously.' 'That,' he concludes triumphantly, 'is axiomatic' (299). A collateral axiom of Nietzsche's sums up Hurree's statistical logic even better: 'It is the iron hand of necessity that throws the dice of chance.'[25]

Managing a necessity that escapes exact control requires a mobile kind of strategic engagement and disengagement, which in the novel goes under the rubric of the 'Great Game.' Everybody in *Kim* plays the Great Game, a political metaphor that Kipling takes from Arthur Conolly's *Journey to the North of India* (1838). A chess player, Conolly used the metaphor as a tool to explain Russian diplomatic maneuvers within a superpower economy and over a particular terrain, India.[26] But Kipling does not restrict English activity to a sequence of chess moves. In *Kim* he clearly has in mind a 'game' that does not involve an open phalanx-to-phalanx confrontation, as in chess. Commentators tend to assume that Kipling works from the model of chess (which is, after all, a traditional diplomatic metaphor, one favored by Clausewitz in the nineteenth century and still employed by Russian diplomats today), when in fact he has a rather different game in mind. In *A Thousand Plateaus* Deleuze and Guattari locate the difference and identify another conceptual model, that of 'Go': 'Chess is a game of State, or of the court: the emperor of China played it. Chess pieces are coded; they have an internal nature from which their movements, situations, and confrontations derive.' Go pieces, in contrast, 'are pellets, disks, simple arithmetic units, and have only an anonymous, collective, or third-person function . . . with no intrinsic properties, only situational ones.' Chess represents a regulated war with front and rear echelons, while 'what is proper to Go is war without battle lines, with neither confrontation nor retreat, without battles even: pure strategy, whereas chess is a semiology.'[27]

Kipling's Great Game inhabits precisely this open space of insertion and situation. Trained in surveying, Kim learns to 'carry pictures in thine eye' (166) instead of writing them down. He belongs not to a written but to an oral culture of surveillance, a world in which the surveillance of space entails the freeing up of time (he always insists that 'my time is given to me without question' [190]), a world in which instrumentation no longer requires instruments. Instead 'a boy would do well to know the precise length of his own foot-pace, so that when he was deprived of what Hurree Chunder called 'adventitious aids,' he might still tread his distances' (166). Kim works, in other words, within the domain not of actual but of potential borders, moving along a laminar flow in a game that 'runs like a shuttle throughout all Hind' (190). And it turns out that the reason the Russians lose Tibet is that they are playing a closed game. While the Russian expedition to Tibet attempts to survey it, the English traverse it without maps and with the collaboration of indigenes. While the Russians take geography as their model, the English take demography and follow the shifting flow of populations, moving from village to village, encampment to encampment. Perhaps the clearest sign of Kim's maturation as a state nomad comes when he throws the kit containing all the Russian survey instruments into a deep Himalayan chasm. With these instruments go Montgomerie's strategies, which, had Kim attempted to hold onto them past their prime, would have exposed him to certain detection. In Tibet the English will maintain hegemony not through instrumentation but through comprehensive knowledge of peoples, and toward this end, during his apprenticeship to Lurgan Sahib, Kim memorizes not mathematical equations (those he gets at St Xavier's), but the whole of the Koran, the names and properties of medicinal drugs, the cadences of a hundred prayers, and the lilt of a dozen *patois*. Finally Lurgan Sahib teaches him a miniature version of the Great Game, the Jewel Game, in which Kim must learn to see fragments as part of a possible whole, a whole nevertheless 'so large that one sees but little at a time' (217).

In *Kim* the crystallized image of the comprehensive knowledge upon which English hegemony rests is the museum, and the 'Wonder House' frames the beginning and end of Kipling's narrative in a variety of ways. From the outset the Lama's expressed wish is that Kim become a museum curator, and the novel ends by placing the Lama squarely within the confines of the museum, for in his enlightened state he reminds Kipling of 'the stone Bodhishat who looks down the patent self-registering turnstiles of the Lahore museum' (336) – a sort of patron saint of the census. But the Lahore Museum must not be mistaken for its metropole, the British Museum. Though certainly a member of the loose confederation of knowledge-producing state apparatuses that has been called the imperial archive, the Lahore Museum contains only local knowledge pertaining to a limited zone of empire. Given up to 'Indian arts and manufactures,' the Lahore Museum comprehends only 'the things that men made in their own province and elsewhere [in India]' (52). This practical autonomy is precisely the source of its effectiveness throughout Kipling's novel. The novel presents the autonomous museum as the British alternative to Tsarist Russia's notorious and failed policy of 'Russification,' according to which hegemony was to be established and maintained through cultural homogeneity.[28] Rather the museum, like the Secret Service itself, operates through a strategy of heterogeneity that takes as its ideal the perfect mobility of human resources and the unobstructed dissemination of information. In *Kim* the most effective museums are not formal syntheses of knowledge but informal amalgamations characterized by bric-à-brac. Kim instantly recognizes that Lurgan Sahib's clearing-house for spies 'is like a Wonder House' that contains even 'more wonders – ghost-daggers and prayer-wheels from Tibet; turquoise and raw amber necklaces; green jade bangles; curiously packed incense-sticks in jars crusted over with raw garnets.' It even contains 'Russian samovars with turquoises on the lid' (200). These wonders do not represent a takeover of the museum by military intelligence so much as they signal, in Paul Virilio's words, the formation of a society whose 'system of military security goes along with its system of social security.'[29] The India Survey is not a front (in the nineteenth-century sense of a façade) but a popular front (in the twentieth-century sense of a politico-military organization coextensive with a population).

In *Kim*, then, social knowledge has become coextensive with military intelligence, and though it may not be possible to place that knowledge in one state archive and classify it methodically, it yet remains possible for one state archivist, one archival superman, provisionally to comprehend all of it. That high archivist is Colonel Creighton, head of the Ethnographic Survey and chief of the Secret Service in India, who is perhaps the most cybernetic character in Victorian literature.[30] It is Creighton who prescribes 'what must be known by Us' (230). Creighton surveys the road, oversees justice, interprets prophecy, supervises the regiment, and superintends the Great Game – but, remarkably, he does not plan anything. He prefers situations to plans, and the game he plays exists primarily as a series of simulations. We never know exactly what he will do with what he knows. An invasion or confrontation may take place, or it may not. The 'information received' may lead to something, or it may not. Like the tactical foray around which Norman Mailer later structures *The Naked and the Dead* (1948), the whole of the game may be an elaborate decoy. Or like the final scene of *Raiders of the Lost Ark* (1981), when workers place the ark of the covenant in a vast warehouse, Creighton may place sensitive information in a place where it will be conveniently 'lost' (more than once Kipling implies that this is exactly what happens to many reports filed at the Secret Service). At no point, in fact, does Creighton do anything that would alter even slightly the existing balance of power. He works not from a dynamic but from a homeostatic model of knowledge, and though he largely manifests this by working to preserve the balance of power in northeast India, he also keeps up a telling interest in scientific experiments that explore the state of physiological equilibrium produced by a balance of functions within organisms (at times he yearns to 'move among spectroscopic experiments, the lesser plants of the frozen tundras, electric flight-measuring machines, and apparatuses for slicing into fractional millimeters the left eye of the female mosquito' [223]). Though everything in the novel takes place under 'the sign of War' (128) it is the sign of war that is not yet war, the sign of a permanent state of emergency, the sign of a state apparatus maintaining political equilibrium, the sign of what Virilio has called 'the passage from wartime to the war of peacetime.' This is the Cold War, a war without heat because it is a war without friction, a peacetime war fully present in *Kim*, a novel in which the calculations of pure strategy entail and provoke almost no violence.[31]

For many years Kipling's ideal of maintaining military control without using force informed and pervaded the British high command. *Kim* appeared in 1901, but, because of the Boer War, Creighton's model of pervasive nonintervention had begun to break down. In the summer of 1902 Lord Curzon, viceroy of India, arrived at a new strategic calculation, according to which the Tsarist Empire was advancing eastward at the rate of some fifty-five square miles a day. Almost immediately this imagined line of advance became the linchpin of English policy in the area. The long history of Russian activity in the region was immediately reformulated to conform to the new conceptual model of automated advance.[32] In one fell swoop the maneuvers of small groups of spies like the one superintended by Creighton became demographically insignificant, and a crisis locked into place. A British 'mission' to Tibet arrived at the border in July 1903, crossed it in December, and occupied Lhasa in August 1904. A chapter title in Austine Waddell's *Lhasa and Its Mysteries, With a Record of the British Tibetan Expedition of 1903–1904* (1905) captures this inexorable logic of movement whereby the sheer momentum of motion was transformed into the applied force of invasion: 'Forward! The Peaceful Mission Becomes an Armed Force.'[33] This logic of advance was the logic of what has come to be called a pre-emptive strike – a strike intended to wipe out, not a population or a polity, but the possibility of an enemy counterstrike. In such a strike the actual occupation of territory is never at issue, and in actual fact the Anglo-Russian Convention of 1907 stipulated that Tibet be removed from international circulation; except by arrangement between England and Russia, scientific expeditions were barred from entering Tibet for three years. Tibet had been traversed by pundits and reduced to a relief map, infiltrated by spies in search of other spies, encroached upon and finally invaded, and now, by provision of treaty, it had been formally relegated to the horizon of knowledge, 'lost' by fiat. Though mapped, Tibet now disappeared from the map, nationally dislocated, transformed into an international reservation for potential knowledge accessible only to the disinterested. A utopian space of comprehensive knowledge had been lost, but after a brief interregnum it would again be found, perfectly preserved, an archive-state under a bell jar at the roof of the world.

III

Tibet became an archive-state at the very moment in history when the Victorian alliance between state and archive was breaking apart. Under the imaginary rubric of the imperial archive, Britain had devised a mythology of knowledge that played a global role in consolidating the British Empire as a secure symbiosis of knowledge and power. Britain began producing representations of the Tibetan state as a utopian archive just as, in the 1930s, the incipient forces of decolonization and total war (theorized by German fascists but first put into practice by the Japanese at Shanghai in 1932) had begun to reconfigure the relation between knowledge and the state, a world in which particular state monopolies over knowledge no longer facilitated but actively impeded the flow of information. The forced reconsolidation of the Victorian project of comprehensive knowledge as an embattled utopian space situated in Tibet signals the breakdown of the imagined global system for information retrieval within the British Empire that has been called the imperial archive.

The Japanese attack on Shanghai in 1932 took immediate shape within British imperialist discourse. The first wave of Japanese bombers approached Shanghai at four o'clock on the morning of 28 January 1932. Flying in staggered formation, the bombers avoided the British, French, Italian, and American zones of this divided city, the world's first internationally sectored urban center, the model for postwar Berlin.[34] Instead they closed on the thickly populated Chapei region north of the city, a residential region under Chinese control. Through their economic policies the Japanese had already done their best to create unemployment as well as food supply and sanitation problems in this sector. Now they struck according to the principle newly laid out by Guilio Drouhet in his enormously influential *The Command of the Air* (1932): they attacked not military installations but centers of population. To shatter civilian morale the Japanese forces took as their epicenter of attack a cultural site, the Commercial Press, the sole source of schoolbooks for a very large part of China and the location of a library of Chinese books, ancient and modern. Along with most other buildings in the sector, the library burned to the ground. The international outcry was immediate and prolonged, for the Shanghai bombing had inaugurated the era of what Field Marshal Erich Ludendorff was the first to call 'totalitarian war,' a phrase he later shortened to the title of his 1935 book *Total War*.

Total war is telluric war, environmental war waged against the earth and its populations. It aims at making insecurity complete, at widening the theater of conflict until it becomes indistinguishable from the globe itself. The First World War, as Ludendorff had recognized, had been a *world* war because 'it was impossible to distinguish where the sphere of the Army and Navy began, and that of the people ended. Army and people were one.' But the First World War had also been a striated war that took place along a more or less immobile grid of front and rear echelons. Beginning in 1932 war now rose above the trenches and extended 'in every sense of the word over the whole territory of the belligerent nations.'[35] It extended, in other words, into the air. A hundred years earlier David Ricardo had observed that air could not be sold because it could not be divided and occupied; now the air became property subject to seizure by states possessing airborne systems of transit and transmission.[36] Launched from distant aircraft carriers, total war encompassed all ground territory yet occupied none. The inhabitants of Shanghai were the first besieged population in history who literally had nowhere to go. They were not surrounded; they could not surrender. They could not even become refugees, for wherever they went the Japanese had seen to it that there was war.

James Hilton's *Lost Horizon* (1933) must be situated within the zone of total war created by the Shanghai bombing. The narrative begins with a conversation in Berlin's Tempelhof airport, the seat of Hermann Goering's Luftwaffe, the organization that extended and perfected the techniques of total war at Guernica in 1937, London in 1940, and Stalingrad in 1942. Almost immediately the narrative cuts to Baskul, a zone of evacuation in an area of the world subject, like Shanghai, to the onslaught of total war. Here, as in André Malraux's *Man's Fate*, also written in 1933 in the wake of the Shanghai bombing (Malraux writes of an attendant 'Shanghai insurrection'), total war is not waged by the state but against it, taking not the explosive form of aerial bombardment but rather the implosive form of uncontrollable internal revolution. The focus of total war, however, remains aerial, and in Hilton's novel a small group of British functionaries and Western nationals find themselves awaiting evacuation in an airport. In all of Peshawar, the only locus of high security left is the airport. At different points in history states have always been closely allied with channels of protection, exchange, and communication such as forts, harbors, and train stations. Hilton presents the airport as just such a conical space capable of reducing the political circulation of bodies and information to a manageable minimum. There British officials can spend their last few moments in Baskul in relative peace, 'packing and destroying documents.'[37] All round them state control has failed, public safety has eroded, and the threat of terror has increased (they remark how 'the revolutionaries were torturing their captives to get information' [66]), but the airport remains inviolate to the bitter end. When the plane finally takes off, its passengers breathe a sigh of relief, for they think they have escaped a country in which a cadre of revolutionaries has transformed an entire population into prisoners of total war.

Once in the air they enter an entirely different space of territoriality. A diptych from *The Geography of World Air Transport* (1944) shows what a defamiliarizing impact flying had on hemispheric travel (Figures 1 and 2). On the surface map the land masses provide fixity; on the air-age map there are only cities – cities, that is, that are virtually synonymous with states. To take an airplane journey between cities is necessarily to pass from one point of intensely regulated state control to another.[38] Even hijackings take place between polities, as the passengers evacuated in a special plane commandeered from the India Survey (where else?) soon learn. For a time the refugees exist in a pure state of abduction; as displaced persons without a destination, they must resign themselves to mobile captivity. The passengers immediately assume that they are chance victims, 'kidnapped for ransom' (27), pawns in a struggle between states. Even the remarkable cooperation of a tribe of nomads during a refueling stop (far and away the most memorable scene in the 1937 film) apparently serves some invisible state design: 'A swarm of bearded tribesmen came forward from all directions, surrounding the machine and effectively preventing any one from

THE PRINCIPAL HEMISPHERE
Surface Map

THE PRINCIPAL HEMISPHERE
Air-Age Map

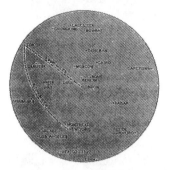

By sea New York is 1500 statute miles nearer Tokyo than is London.

(Routes as drawn above show shortest direct airline courses on this type of projection).
By air New York is 800 miles farther away from Tokyo than is London.

Figures 1 and 2. "Surface Map" and "Air-Age Map" of the "Principal Hemisphere." From J. Parker Van Zandt, *The Geography of World Air Transport* (Washington, D.C., 1944), 6–7.

getting out except the pilot. . . . Meanwhile cans of gasoline were fetched from a dump close by, and emptied into the exceptionally capacious tanks' (26). As the plane takes off again, the chief British functionary, Conway, directs his gaze at a mountain range 'merging toward the west in a horizon.' The horizon he sees receding from the plane window is the apparent intersection of the earth and sky as seen by an observer. To fix this relativistic horizon in Newtonian space and time and to restore the lost horizontality of the air-age map, Conway quickly resorts to an actuarial mode of perception, 'envisioning maps, calculating distances, estimating times and speeds' (37–8). But the truth is that he has no idea where he is. Outside of the constructed corridors of air travel, space seems deformed into 'something raw and monstrous' and time seems to stand still, 'floating' in a disembodied vision of hallucinatory clarity (37).

Even unmapped space, however, has its regime of security, and after a bumpy landing the DC-3's passengers find themselves deposited at the gateway to a hieratic archive-state. At Shangri-La another

lost horizon – the ever-receding horizon of comprehensive knowledge – replaces the imagined intersection of earth and sky. The
architectonics of Tibetan Shangri-La offer the contemplative Conway a demilitarized zone of utopian knowledge: a place, as Georges
Bataille has shown, where military security is so complete that it can
afford to do without armies and devote itself wholly to the life of the
mind.[39] Hilton presents that life as the very embodiment of both the
material and human components of the Victorian archive. The
building contains 'treasures that museums and millionaires alike
would have bargained for,' including 'the world's best literature'
and 'a great deal of abstruse and curious stuff' (94–5). The building's inhabitants, as Conway tells the head monk, are 'specimen[s] in
your museum of antiquities' (157). Neither outpost nor metropole,
Shangri-La is a museum that has adapted itself to a Himalayan
environment that most nineteenth-century scientists interpreted as
evidence of a geological deluge. Shangri-La is a high command, a
'central intelligence' (177), in a land considered militarily uninhabi-
table. It does not take Conway long to realize that the flight from
Baskul had been 'something planned, prepared, and carried out at
the instigation of Shangri-La.' Everything points to the designs of a
high command, 'to a high directing intelligence bent upon its own
purposes; there had been, as it were, a single arch of intentions
spanning the inexplicable hours and minutes. But what *was* that
intention?' (104).

The answer to this question occupies the rest of the novel, which
spells out the High Lama's strategic conception of the utopian
archive. The High Lama views his utopia essentially as a fortress.
Developed by Sebastien de Vauban in the seventeenth century, the
fortress was a highly formalized technology making use of fortifications, trenches, and earthworks to protect major cities.[40] It rested on
the idea that the main line of military defense should be placed
outside the fortress, allowing the fortress itself to remain an essentially civilian enclosure. By using detached exterior defenses he
essentially constructed an artificial mountain range so daunting that
no enemy would attempt to penetrate it. In the same way, the High
Lama's utopian archive is a space of state knowledge that is defens-
ible from a military point of view; protected by an impenetrable
escarpment of mountains (citing the example of Hannibal, Clausewitz had advised against mountain warfare), it exists primarily to

survive total war. The Lama explicitly foresees a conflagration 'as the world has not seen before. There will be no safety by arms, no help from authority, no answer in science. It will rage till every flower of culture is trampled, and all human things are leveled in a vast chaos' (199). The only hope rests with those who are 'too secret to be found or too humble to be noticed. And Shangri-La may hope to be both of these. The airman bearing loads of death to the great cities will not pass our way, and if by chance he should he may not consider us worth a bomb' (199). The utopian archive at Shangri-La is thus a survivalist archive, an archive 'hidden behind the mountains in the valley of the Blue Moon,' an archive to be 'preserved as by miracle for a new Renaissance' (199). So perfectly protected is the interior of the fortress archive that it can afford to be moderate (the key word both in Vauban's lexicon and in the High Lama's philosophy) and demilitarized (save for the press gang Shangri-La sends out to conscript Conway, and what Lewis Mumford once called the 'iron discipline' present in monasticism itself). Siegecraft, once the art of defending the strategic cities of European states, has become the art of defending the archive.[41]

The structure of Shangri-La, however, does not simply replicate the intention and design of eighteenth-century siegecraft. In Vauban's time siegecraft presupposed a centered power crystalized around a sovereign structure. In Hilton's novel the archive-state at Shangri-La operates not only as a fortress but also as a museum that spreads its capillaries all over the world to recruit the best and the brightest personnel from among the shifting pool of state nomads. Assigned to 'Baskul, Pekin, Makao, and other places,' Conway has 'moved about pretty often' (24). An orientalist, he belongs to the same administrative elite that produced Creighton and trained Kim. As a state nomad Conway displays a characteristic willingness to go with the flow of unfolding events (this infuriates his subaltern, Mallinson); he neither makes decisions nor forms intentions; his power, like Creighton's, is completely invested in its field of application. In seeking out a state nomad like Conway, Shangri-La implicitly acknowledges the weakness of its own fixed position. Aware that Shangri-La has remained safe merely because its location has not been divulged, the High Lama seeks a replacement who, in the classic terms of the imperial archive, will be capable of negotiating the fluctuating threshold between local and global knowledges.

The High Lama has succeeded so far only because Tibet had been demarcated as an international zone of inaccessible knowledge. Much of the novel turns on the High Lama's effort to convince Conway that a fortress archive with a state nomad in command will be able to withstand the onslaught of modern war. Each of Conway's companions contributes in some way to the project of modernizing Shangri-La – one by installing plumbing, another by opening a mission. Before long the central question of the book becomes one asked frequently by European states during the 1930s: will the state be able to modernize quickly enough (generally by developing and deploying nomadic military technologies such as tanks and aircraft) to survive the coming conflict? Like *Kim, Lost Horizon* offers a composite portrait of the nomadization of archival intelligence; not Kipling's positive portrait that shows the success of a fluid positionality of multiple knowledges, but a negative portrait that dramatizes (and sentimentalizes) the epistemological failure of the archive–state synthesis, a failure emblematized in Shangri-La's failure to recruit Conway for the position of High Lama.

The great conundrum about *Lost Horizon*, then, equally pressing in both novel and film versions, is why Conway is so easily persuaded to leave the utopian archive when, as he himself admits, he has fully assented to the High Lama's utopian vision of sentimental survivalism.[42] Without question Hilton and Hollywood also assent; Hilton embodies criticism of Shangri-La in the figure of Mallinson, a lineal descendant of the racist drummer boy in *Kim* and the prejudiced subaltern Ronny in *A Passage to India* (1924), while in 1973 Hollywood manages to convert the story into a euphoric Burt Bacharach musical. Yet the utopian archive has its limitations. The lamas of Shangri-La counter the coming apocalypse with nothing more than the dictatorship of the infirm (the survival of the fittest has become, quite simply, survival), a colony of superannuated dilettantes presiding over a seemingly well-preserved Victorian archive. Our first impression is that Shangri-La is a haven of 'lost' knowledge of precisely the kind that fascinated nineteenth-century museums preoccupied with reconstructing the roots of lost languages, tracing the origin of the species, tracking down the ten tribes of Israel, and locating the source of the Nile (one of the monks actually teaches Conway a lost Chopin sonata). But the monks

Conway meets at Shangri-La are more like taxidermists than ency-
clopedists; they do not attempt to construct hegemonic modes of
cognition that comprehend all knowledge so much as superintend a
few fragments, 'tideless channels in which they dived in mere
waywardness, retrieving, like Briac, fragments of old tunes, or like
the English ex-curate, a new theory about *Wuthering Heights*' (190–
91). Like today's desperate efforts by environmentalists to preserve a
few representative members of chronically endangered species, the
result is not comprehensive knowledge but a few fragments shored
against the ruins, an essentially modern vision of a Victorian archive
preserved not so much to some particular end (the High Lama comes
right out and says that after the apocalypse, 'my vision weakens'
[100]), as for the sake of survival itself. In the final analysis Hilton's
novel must be regarded as a sentimental representation of the
Victorian archive, an imperialist nostalgia for a kind of comprehensive knowledge that had once seemed attainable within the empire's
mythology of knowledge. Recall that in the nineteenth century the
imperial archive succeeded not in attaining comprehensive knowledge but in collectively imagining a not-too-distant future when all
species would be identified, all languages translated, all books
catalogued. *Lost Horizon* is the perfect title for Hilton's project, for
it does not imply a nostalgia for something that was held and then
lost, but rather a nostalgia for a goal that once appeared on the
horizon of possibility and then was lost from sight, a lost horizon of
comprehensive knowledge.

Hilton's utopian archive will resort to almost any expedient to
maintain this illusion of encyclopedic totality. Shangri-La drugs its
postulants, subjects its Tibetan indigenes to forced labor, and offers
asylum beyond the range of extradition to criminals. From the
moment Conway arrives at Shangri-La he suspects that he is being
drugged. 'He suspected, too, that [his first meal] might have contained some herb or drug to relieve respiration, for he not only felt a
difference himself, but could observe a greater ease among his fellow
guests' (70). Later, 'something in his voice, as well as in his bodily
sensations, gave Conway a renewed impression that he had been
slightly doped' (75). Soon he hardly notices the addiction: 'As
Conway continued to gaze, a deeper repose overspread him' (80).
And though Hilton avoids the issue, Shangri-La has been colonized
by an elite group of Westerners who establish a hieratic order

'whose best subjects, undoubtedly, are the Nordic and Latin races of Europe' (151). This is utopia as latifundium, where the indigenes work the fields and mines and serve as the recipients of various philanthropic projects initiated by the monks. This monastic order cultivates the life of the mind in the manner of a narcotic product (like Chinese opium, Mexican marijuana, Panamanian cocaine, or Afghan hashish) that it plans to export to the rest of the world, supplying it at just the right time with what the High Lama calls 'the fragrance of our history' (151). Leaving utopia naturally means undergoing withdrawal, which is exactly what happens to the girl whom Mallinson spirits away; she goes into a rapid state of decline. Accessible only by means of a kind of Ho Chi Minh Trail (the porters who keep Shangri-La supplied with Western goods evade tariff, keep its location secret, yield to bribery, and are clearly smugglers), Shangri-La is also a kind of criminal lair, as Hilton tacitly acknowledges when he includes an American swindler, Chalmers Bryant, among the party of hijacked passengers (Bryant of course decides to stay put). Under these circumstances it is hardly surprising that Conway decides to leave Shangri-La. The utopian archive fails to maintain its hold over him, and the failure of the archive is not only the general failure of the state to totalize knowledge but the particular failure of the state agency of a high command to replace the disorder of the world with a model of exact, or even approximate, knowledge.

If in the final analysis *Lost Horizon* chronicles the breakdown of the narrative of the high command, it also details the replacement of the high command narrative of *Kim* by the narrative of the contingency plan. More than anything else, Shangri-La is a contingency plan, one hundred and fifty years in the making, that presupposes the failure of the high command and is designed to reconstitute state authority by redirecting it into other channels. In twentieth-century discourse the state nomad is neither a military geographer like Montgomerie, who uses local means to generate local knowledge, nor a commander like Creighton, a figure who for all his mobility deals only with Indian affairs, but a contingency planner like Conway, the once and future High Lama of Shangri-La whom Hilton depicts at the novel's end as drifting, deterritorialized, uncertain of nationality, and perhaps incapable of staying in one place. Conway may or may not find the utopian archive; the novel opens and closes with narrators who are not altogether sure whether such a utopian project could even exist in the modern world, and who wonder out loud whether Conway did not just make it all up. In the end it hardly matters, for the question gets lost in the vortex of coming war, war beyond the High Lama's fear of a second Napoleon, beyond his fear of what Thomas Malthus once called 'ordinary destruction,' total war that spares no archives.[43] The novel ends in a complete loss of neutrality for the archive-state. It is now moot whether Conway finds Shangri-La and assumes control over it, for it is transparently clear to the narrator that no archive, and indeed no state, will be able to evade or withstand the coming conflagration. The utopian archive, the last preserve of total state control over knowledge, has finally become a hierarchy of forms without content, a center without central intelligence, a control room without control.

It would be a mistake, however, to see the failure of Hilton's utopian construction of the archive as a complete failure of the Victorian imperial archive, with its microepistemological project of national security. The utopian archive must finally be seen as an ideological construct that Hilton has imposed on the construction of state power. By a neat operation the High Lama represents the 'knowledge' he seeks to preserve in a fortress as a macroepistemology that does not include the knowledge of war. Born in the eighteenth century, the High Lama instructs that Shangri-La use no technology beyond that which can be found in Diderot's *Encyclopedia*, choosing to forgo what Conway, in a clear echo of Butler's *Erewhon*, calls 'the fatal knowledge of machinery' (72).[44] The systems failure that plagues Shangri-La at the end of Hilton's novel must be seen as signaling not the end of the archive, which was hardly utopian as conceived by a Montgomerie or a Creighton, but rather its adjustment from a global to a local representation of comprehensive knowledge. The imperial archive had predicated its mythology of knowledges on the assumption that the local was included in the global; Shangri-La bases its enterprise on the contrary assumption that the global was included in the local, the marginal, the forgotten, in preparation for the day when Western culture can move once again into an encompassing and hegemonic configuration. A prototype of the global village (by definition, anything 'global' is Western), Shangri-La is a space of knowledge out of which state control over knowledge – complete with its law, order, stability, and closure – can reassert itself in a post-apocalyptic world.[45]

Almost immediately after the book's publication, 'Shangri-La' took its place among the great modern myths of knowledge because it performed a simple but drastic operation: it represented an archive achieved and maintained by the state (here, explicitly as a state) without recourse to military force. This myth of archive and utopia had to be revised during World War II, when American military censors edited the film version to cut out the Lama's vision of the nonviolent archive-state. In a rudimentary way the High Lama seems to realize that he is trying to construct a state without an army in a world where states with armies press inward from all directions at total war with one another. Again and again he characterizes the force of states as forms of interference in the global epistemology he imagines will arise out of the ruins.[46] The Lama believes that the violence inherent in states prevents the final totalization and unification of knowledge – to the degree that it exists at all, total knowledge now equals total war, an equation encoded in our term 'information explosion' – and in his monologues he offers no epistemology that represents anything like a complete organization of comprehensive knowledge. A product of the 1930s, Hilton's High Lama thinks of knowledge less in terms of order and mastery than in terms of chance and entropy. For the Lama the world remains unified, no longer by an organizational system like geography but by the omnipresence of disorganization, disorder, entropy – on a global scale. The Lama speaks not of regional but of global disorder; outside of the utopian archive there exists only entropy. In *Lost Horizon*, the end of the world must be seen as a corollary of the idea of a single world unified by information. Like Oswald Spengler, whom he echoes at several points, the Lama must be regarded as a prophet of global entropy.[47]

The 1920s and 1930s were full of narratives detailing the end of the world. These were epistemological epics dealing less with the end of the physical world than with the end of the Victorian mythology of the world structured as a secure global symbiosis of knowledge and state power. To many, the end of the Victorian archive must have looked like the end of the world as they knew it. Pre-atomic novels such as Edward Shank's *People of the Ruins* (1920), P.A.

Graham's *The Collapse of Homo Sapiens* (1923), and John Gloag's *Tomorrow's Yesterday* (1932) seem weak to us today because they take as their premiss not the ecological destruction of the planet but the breakdown of the Victorian apparatus for legitimating knowledge. The primacy of the imaginary state apparatus that has been termed the imperial archive has eroded; contingency plans have failed; the limits of state intervention emerge in stark clarity. The imperial archive survives only as the unity of a utopia superintended by intellectuals. In an uncanny way Hilton's novel anticipates the conclusions Karl Mannheim reached a few years later in *Ideology and Utopia* (1936). Like so many of his contemporaries, Mannheim claims that no one theory can possibly achieve a comprehensive knowledge of the world (under what he calls 'relationism' all theories of knowledge articulate specific class positions and ideologies). But he also argues that 'a free-floating intelligentsia' can transcend its members' social origins and harmoniously integrate their perspectives into a complete and measured knowledge of the world. Like Hilton, Mannheim preserves the project of comprehensive knowledge as the assigned province of an intellectual mandarinate, a universal class whose aim would be 'the discovery of a position from which a total perspective would be possible' so that 'they might play the part of watchmen in what otherwise might be a pitch-black night.' As in Shangri-La, the intellectuals' disinterested concern for the whole world foretells an end to social conflict, or at least enables a cultured elite to survive the suicide pact of states.[48]

This bleak scenario, in which states destroy each other and threaten the destruction of all knowledge, would seem to resolve once and for all the problem of the relation of knowledge to the state. But the problem did not simply disappear with the demise of the Victorian mythology of knowledge channeled unimpeded to the state. For sixty years the Victorian archive had been widely regarded as the imperial equivalent of the bourgeois public sphere; it presupposed the neutrality and instrumentality of all communicative networks at the same time as it formed and channeled knowledge within epistemological networks specific to a class, a state, and a nation.[49] The breakdown of the Victorian archive must be seen as the end of the imperial public sphere, an open system of knowledges characterized by the cooperative interplay of the great European powers. After World War II the power of information control formerly attributed to the state in the imperial archive would begin to be attributed to technology (as in the media epistemology of Marshall McLuhan), to institutional infrastructures (as in the archeology of Michel Foucault), to language (as in structuralist poetics), to corporations (as in the novels of Thomas Pynchon), to states removed to other planets (as in 1950s science fiction), even to the structure of information itself (as in the fantasias of various information theorists).[50] Far from disappearing into the mists of the Himalayas, the imperatives of the Victorian imperial mythology of knowledge continue to animate the production of knowledge as a utopian epistemology, a disposition to comprehensive knowledge, and a will to power. The archive, the sum total of the known and knowable that once seemed an attainable goal hovering on the horizon of possibility, became and has remained utopia.

TWO

ARCHIVE AND FORM

This chapter is about the place of monstrosity in the nineteenth-century imperial imagination. Until Bram Stoker's *Dracula*, there are few monsters in Victorian fiction. In Victorian literature ghosts, those images of a nether world replete with human significance, are more common than monsters, and it is worth asking why. Victorian travellers like Richard Burton and Henry Stanley never saw monsters. In his *Voyage of the Beagle* (1831–36) Darwin travelled around the world without seeing one. Thomas Henry Huxley doubted whether monsters ever existed, even in the distant past. In Poe 'monstrous' is always an adjective, never a noun, and monstrosity resides in the behavioral perversions of the self, as it does in Lombroso, where the monster is the criminal. In Victorian gothic it is the natural landscape that is monstrous. Even in the murky world of imperial gothic, as in Haggard's *She* (1887), there are no monsters of nature save for a woman who lives on eternally in a dead city. Why are there no monsters in Victorian literature?

This chapter looks at the role the science of form, or morphology, played in imagining a unitary natural world in which there would no longer be any place for monstrosity. Throughout the nineteenth century the practice of biology relied overwhelmingly on the techniques of morphology, the science concerned with the problems of form, function, and transformation in matter.[1] The immediate heirs to the work of the great taxonomists of the eighteenth century, the Victorian morphologists saw all life as an organized succession of forms capable of being derived from a unitary apparatus of constants and variables. The nineteenth-century and early-twentieth-century morphology of Owen and Darwin and D'Arcy Thompson represented life as unfolding within a Cartesian mechanism of vectors and coordinates, but it also moved the old Linnaean hierarchies into a new and completely different register. It fashioned not a hierarchy of general forms but a lineage of specific ones. No less an authority than Auguste Comte located the discipline of morphology perfectly at the juncture of the general and the particular, the abstract and the concrete.[2] In morphology the project of a complete and unravelled representation of existence became the ally of the positivist project of comprehensive knowledge. More than anything else, the work of morphology was to construct lines to join together the established points of positive knowledge into a projected network of comprehensive knowledge; for many years there was nothing in the geological record linking *mesopithecus* and *homo sapiens* but the fictions of morphology. A method for locating continuity within discontinuity, morphology provided filler for the great gaps of knowledge the Victorians were continually discovering in their own global schemes. Morphology put all beings on the same imperial family tree. In the heyday of Victorian morphology, there were no longer any singular beings in the universe other than those which human beings created for themselves; as in Mary Shelley's novel, the Victorian monster is made, not born. Even ghosts, as in James's *Turn of the Screw* (1898), came to be seen less as independent beings than as projections of human psychology. The Victorian morphologists shared a common conviction that the day was coming when the relationship of all living beings could be traced in a great common genealogy. When that day came, there would no longer be any creature unable to fit anywhere on the great chain of beings. The Victorian search for the mythical 'missing link' presaged not so much a new kind of monster as an end to all monstrosity. The search for the missing link was the search for the final link in the evolutionary chain. At the point at which the missing link shored up the great chain once and for all, nothing could ever be monstrous again because everything would then be known, fixed in a continuous reconstruction of serial descent.

Victorian morphology saw its origins in certain debates about natural form going back to the eighteenth century. The science of form began as an explicitly universal science devoted to the task of preparing scientific directories of the natural world. In his *Systema naturae* (1735) Linnaeus uses an empirical method of nomination to construct an ideal taxonomy of pure forms. He claims to include all known species of plants, but he also advances the idea that the study of matter can be anchored in philosophical first principles. The problem of form was to be solved by constructing a calculus of four variables in which 'every note should be a product of number, of form, of proportion, of situation.'[3] Linnaeus did everything he could to construct a work of natural history without undertaking to write an actual history of nature. For him nature always made manifest certain irreducible forms of order, forms which he attempted to call forth using an intricate system of symbols that resembled magic characters. Despite this emphasis on nature as a self-contained structure – what came to be called 'the natural order' – natural form tended most easily to assume the form of logic, and his conception of the wholeness of nature assumed that nature would always somehow resolve itself into a synchronic logical arrangement. Form in Linnaeus meant taxidermy; single specimens in little boxes defined in terms of one generalized rubric, however defined. Any form that fell outside the purview of the logical definition was, by definition, a singularity, a fluke, a freak of nature, and the best that could be done was to place it in a bottomless category for all the deviations from logic traversed by nature, the special category of the monstrous.

In the nineteenth century the Linnaean metaphysics of the fixed form, the *forma formata*, gave way to the new field of the changing form, the *forma formans*. The problem of form no longer entailed the tabulation of synchronies; it now began to be equated with the diachronic reconstruction of lines of formal development. Linnaeus believed that since the forms of living beings were fixed, he did not need to delve into the past to study them. The new evolutionary reconstruction, however, extended into the past, the past of the fossil record. The fossil record equipped biology with a historical archive potentially capable of accounting for every form that had ever existed; all the exceptions that the old taxonomies had once relegated to the category of the monstrous could theoretically be rehabilitated using the new historical method in morphology. Just as, within philology, the desire to understand living languages led to a fixation on dead languages, in morphology the desire to understand living matter led to the residues of the fossil record. Victorian texts abound in representations of decaying residues, and in a classic morphological text, *The Formation of Vegetable Mould through the*

Action of Worms (1881) Darwin would go so far as to attribute the life of the earth's topsoil to an ecology saturated with decomposing residues. In a great variety of ways the new nineteenth-century morphology was most concerned with constructing a lineage not of the present but of the past. The creatures that evolution had passed by were strange at first but, safely dead, they could be easily domesticated. Unearthed as fragments of bone, they became skulls and spines reconstructed in some museum of natural history, no longer monstrous, little capable of inspiring fear or awe, not warnings or portents but destinations for family outings, dinosaurs for children. Life on earth was always changing, and once you knew how to follow out the changes throughout all time, there would be no monsters save somewhere in the past, buried in the vast geological archive of the fossil record.

In the course of the nineteenth century it became clear that there was no longer any place for monstrosity within the biology of living matter. If the motto of Renaissance humanism was 'nothing human is alien,' the motto of Victorian morphology now became 'nothing alive is alien.' There was a confidence that all forms, however monstrous they might at first appear to the examining eye, would at last be discovered to be related by serial descent to other, less alien forms. Deviations from normative forms could now be explained merely by adjusting the focus of a historical reconstruction. Monsters, once considered singular forms, were now placed in active relation to other forms, whether presently living or long dead. The order of things went from being the order of ordered things to being the order of all things that had ever existed. Thus did the one characteristic move of all formal explanation in the nineteenth century – the ranking of all species by historical descent and modification – wipe out in one broad stroke the conditions of possibility for the stores of monsters that had once abounded in texts of literature, travel, natural history, and natural philosophy. Henceforth the forces of monstrosity would have to be located outside the Darwinian world-view, for within it, all monsters were our distant relatives.

This chapter shows that by the turn of the century a new form of monstrosity arose to outwit Darwin. These new monsters were essentially mutants, capable of sudden and catastrophic changes of form, a kind of change outlawed and virtually unknowable under the Darwinian system. Even at the height of Darwinism in late-Victorian Britain, writers began to imagine a great variety of monsters that fell outside the sureties of lineage enshrined in morphology. These monsters were beings capable of sudden changes of form. They were threats to the global claim of Darwinism, disrupting the very order of things and even threatening to bring about the end of Empire. The end was widely figured as a global morphology turned upside down, a state in which monsters that do not follow, and cannot be understood by, the ordinal system of morphological development, disrupt and finally overwhelm the harmonious Darwinian archive of Empire. The functioning British monopoly over knowledge ends in Bram Stoker's *Dracula* (1897), where a colonial alterity comes to be closely aligned with forms refusing to follow the ordinal scheme of historical morphological development. The abiding figure for this representation of morphological alterity is of course the vampire, a figure that first achieved full prominence at the close of the nineteenth century. H.G. Wells also hit on the idea of the mutant in his *Island of Dr. Moreau* (1898), a narrative in which an evil doctor incubates mutants on a remote island. Stoker, however, chose to place his monster in a larger international context and play out the problem of mutation on a much larger scale. He adapted an existing story rather than fabricating a new one, and his powerful new turn on the old Dracula story cannot be understood without a sense of how thoroughly he made his monster violate the doctrines of Darwinian morphology and so turn the natural world upside down. The narrative of *Dracula* makes it clear that there are some species whose origins cannot be understood using the Darwinian model, and that these originless species, impossible according to Darwin, had become the archetypal monsters of the twentieth century. After Dracula the monster stood once again outside science, not safely immured in the descent of man.

In common with the other chapters in this book, what follows has been laid out to trace a cultural course of development running parallel to the imperial trajectory of colonization, occupation, and decolonization. It shows the establishment, failure, and reconsolidation of a variant on the central organizing myth of comprehensive knowledge, the myth of the positive knowledge of form. The first part of the chapter reconstructs the central position which the notion of form occupied in pre-imperial discourse and considers

Lewis Carroll's *Alice in Wonderland* (1865) and *Through the Looking Glass* (1871) as an anatomy of the problem of positive knowledge of exceptional forms within mid-Victorian morphology. The Alice books are about a little girl dropped into a world of monsters, monsters whose world changes in accordance with the dictates of logical form. The second part looks at a fully imperial morphology in a sequence of turn-of-the-century texts and places Bram Stoker's *Dracula* (1897) in the context of morphological theories of monstrosity and decay. The third examines J.G. Ballard's *The Crystal World* (1966), a text that links African decolonization with the rapid spread of an unknown crystalline form, and that testifies to the continuing presence of morphological assumptions in modern British literature. It will be seen that the search for the positive knowledge of form passed, as was the case with so many other positivist projects of comprehensive knowledge in the late nineteenth century, first from the domain of science into the domain of myth, and last into the domain of ideology. Yet at all points it preserved something of the essential character of the Victorian desire for the unification of all knowledge, a squaring of all departments of knowledge into a circle of concordant knowledges. In biology the project of constructing universal taxonomies of form remains very much alive, one of the last surviving emblems of the Victorian imperium, the project of a positive and comprehensive knowledge of the world.

I

For two centuries the science of morphology has worked to dissociate itself from the traditional fictions of metamorphosis. Alterations of form in morphology have none of the overt caprice of transformation in Ovid, where catastrophic changes issue from the summonses of gods. It was only in the nineteenth century that the science of form even began to concern itself with the mechanics of formal transformation. Rather the project of scientific morphology, idealistic or empirical, continuous or discontinuous, deductive or inductive, has always rested on a fundamental assumption of consonant wholeness. The system of form that developed within eighteenth-century botany asserted the priority of the whole, the idea that without the whole the parts are nothing, even as it allowed for the manifestation of growth in the extension of the plant, the assimilation or conversion of materials external to the plant into substances useful to the plant, the shaping of the plant according to the dictates of its own internal plan, and the interdependence between parts as constitutive of the whole plant. So influential was this matrix of organic form that, when Darwin toured South America in the early 1830s, the immense variety of new plant forms he saw, 'plants assuming most fantastical forms,' forms falling outside of all existing structures of forms, scarcely disturbed his center of gravity.[4] He had a confidence that everything would eventually come together with the precision of geometry. All relative magnitudes of formal difference would be subject to explanation by rectilinear coordinates (to make his taxonomies seem less mathematical and more organic, Darwin, like most of his nineteenth-century contemporaries, called them 'trees'). The loss of a complete knowledge of the world was always a temporary matter, for in the fullness of time the whole would be regained.[5]

In some respects, then, the demands of the whole in Darwin remain little changed from the Linnaean hierarchy. To overcome the separatist tendencies in his botanic material, Linnaeus had constructed classes to force variegated evidence into prescribed categories. He saw himself as a kind of technical writer supplying the specifications of a finished and complete product inspired by one logical and uniform Design. For Linnaeus, the form of logic dictated the logic of form, and the weight of design dictated the scale of designation. Though Darwin no longer accepted the argument from logical design, he was far from willing to abolish the typologies of classification derived from it. In fact he wanted to extend them. He devoted a long chapter in *The Origin of Species* (1859) to arguing for a great increase in the number of categories used to classify beings, all the while preserving most of Linnaeus's genera as families or still higher groups and advancing the project of an attainable holistic order.[6] The crucial difference is that the construction of the whole to which Darwin subscribed understood nature as a global rather than a universal totality. Darwin saw nature as the natural *world*. It is worth remembering that while Linnaeus spent his career in the confines of his native Sweden, Darwin began his by circumnavigating the globe. In Linnaean nature form is horizontal; it has a name and a position but not a local habitation and a place. In Darwin the project of comprehensive knowledge loses its universal inflection; the world of nature becomes a vertical world, a specific world, a relational world, an instrumental world, above all, a colonial world.

The corollary to the Linnaean postulate of the absolute whole is that such a whole, though it forms a unitary field of order, is not ordinally manipulable. The claim to certainty that Linnaean order makes is, purely and simply, a claim to the inherent certainty of order. The purpose of order is not to exert order over non-ordered areas of the world but to infer a universal order from the evidence at hand. Operating as it did by inference and interpolation, Linnaean order had no colonial aspirations whatsoever. Rather, in the eighteenth century the science of form was a particular lineage of the absolutist state. An absolute whole is a conception well suited to the requirements of the absolutist state in which colonies tend to be viewed as subordinate parts of a sovereign whole, as 'new' Englands in which economic and political transformation somehow issue as if by fiat from the numen of the original state. The unitary field of order favored by the absolutist state does not require manipulation to stay ordered, for order is universal and cannot be affected by contingent action. The world does not need to be converted to a new order of Empire for the simple reason that it has already been ordered, at every time and in every place. Form in a colonial world is at best a mutilated copy of form in the metropolitan world.

The sole representation of the colonial within the Linnaean system is the order of the monstrous. Monsters in Linnaeus rise only from the colonial world and display only a contingent alterity. Monsters are figures for alterity outside of European systems of order, an alterity consistently figured as deformation. The monster ensures the placement of difference within the general science of order.[7] The monster is the joker in the Linnaean deck of cards, the undefined addendum, the blind spot in an otherwise compact system of order. In the 1930s the physicist Kurt Gödel offered a simple but convincing explanation for why projects of comprehensive knowledge such as Linnaeus's fail to achieve their ends. Gödel stated simply that a system of axioms cannot encompass all possible variations on that system. It cannot, in other words, foresee which variation will succeed in disturbing the system along its fault lines.[8] The central position of the monster in the eighteenth-century science of form turns out at last to be the Gödel-moment in all taxonomy when the ordering impulse admits its own inexactitude. By resolving irresolution into a category of its own, the monster-category is a tacit admission that all knowledge is neither comprehensive in scope nor logical in form. It is an admission that new and unusual modifications arise from time to time that cannot be derived from a system of systems. As a category it bears silent witness to the existence of unforeseen transformations even as it attempts to lay to rest a much larger problem, the problem of the catastrophic mutation of form.

It was exactly this problem of ordering a disordered nature that led Lewis Carroll, a mathematician whose work on the mathematics of form still commands attention, to construct a lasting burlesque of the general science of ordered form. *Alice in Wonderland* and *Through the Looking Glass* represent form as indomitable. A hundred years after the death of Linnaeus, Carroll's Alice stories laid bare the structure of what had become an obsolete science of form. Carroll structures his fantasy as a questioning of the received categories of morphology by performing a single and striking operation: he links the catastrophic mutation of form to the deconstruction of established logical categories. Unquestionably the most basic feature of the Alice texts is Carroll's linking of logical to natural form. Carroll goes to the end of his wits to make the Linnaean link – the basic assumption of eighteenth-century morphology that the form of logic dictates the logic of form – completely untenable. The mutations that Alice witnesses and undergoes make it impossible to maintain the fidelity of natural to logical form. But Carroll does not restrict his parody to highlighting unaccountable changes in form. Rather, the Alice stories are an anatomy of the very monstrosity of logic itself in dictating form. Logic, the Linnaean logic of form, is the only monster in the Alice books. The shapes the monsters assume there – cards, chessmen, cats – tend toward the domestic and the serene, not the strange and the portentous. Nothing in *Alice in Wonderland* and *Through the Looking Glass* turns out to be more truly monstrous than the operation of logic itself, which dictates shape and configuration at every instant.

Most of Alice's adventures among the beings of Wonderland devolve on reversals of the logical order of common sense. Everything moves in both directions at once, prompting Alice to repeat

like a mantra her pointed question, 'Which way, which way?' Alice
becomes larger and she becomes smaller. She crosses from the day
before to the day after, passing over the present: 'Jam tomorrow and
jam yesterday – but never jam *to-day*.' She reverses more and less, as
when five nights are five times hotter than a single night, 'but they
must be five times as cold for the same reason.' Active and passive
switch positions, as 'do cats eat bats?' becomes 'do bats eat cats?'
And, perhaps most prominently, cause and effect change places as
beings receive punishment before committing crimes, cry before
wounding themselves, and serve food before dividing up the serv-
ings.[9] This series of reversals makes it virtually impossible to group
morphological phenomena into general propositions. In no way
does the surface of things mutate according to some presumed inner
plan; morphology is no longer morpho-logical. Alice cannot perform the two operations most characteristic of the eighteenth-
century science of form: she cannot fix the visible world in stable
logical categories, and just as importantly, she cannot remember her
own name. The loss of the proper name deals a final and crushing
blow to the language of logical morphology, which, more than
anything else, had been founded on the certainty of designation. In
the Alice stories the very possibility of a unitary formulation for the
science of form has become doubtful and remote.

The Alice stories also cast doubt on the certainty of allied absolutist conceptions of order. At all points Carroll makes it clear that
Wonderland is an absolutist state that has lost its bearings. Wonderland is ruled by an imperious Queen who has adopted the cry of the
Terror of the French Revolution, 'Off with their heads!' The state
and the control it exerts are purely a matter of rhetoric; as in
morphology, the absolutist form of order has lost its structural
stability. The dictates of Wonderland's absolutist state are completely unrelated to the world of forms it actually contains. The
Queen has no control over the forms that the beings in her kingdom
assume, for the simple reason that everything in Wonderland is
singular and nothing is repeatable. Form is indomitable, the world is
full of functionless beings. At the croquet game the hedgehogs and
flamingoes and card soldiers do not long retain their functions as
equipment in the game. They take up one function only to relinquish
it quickly and move to another. The croquet game must be seen as a
carnival of form and function, a coming apart of form and a

rebelling against function. In the Alice stories nothing is more fragile than the link joining form to function (unlike the animals in most Victorian children's books, forms do not even begin to assume the functions they actually perform in the natural world). In *Alice in Wonderland* and *Through the Looking Glass* form is at best imperfectly manipulable. The state cannot control it. Carroll sees an excess at the heart of form that unsettles it into a state of measureless mad becoming.

The Alice stories of Lewis Carroll can be taken as a negative picture of the emergence of a Darwinian morphology in mid- and late-Victorian Britain (a positive picture, less devoted to parody of the Linnaean system, can be found in Charles Kingsley's parable of selective metamorphosis, *The Water Babies* [1862–63]). Wonderland is everything that the mid-Victorian project of the positive knowledge of form sought to drive underground once and for all. At all points the Alice stories fail to provide a causal explanation of development. The project of Darwinian morphology rather fixed its sights on the grey areas between forms. It sought to verify the existence of forms between forms. As advanced by Darwin in *The Origin of Species* (1859), and later consolidated by E.S. Russell in *Form and Function* (1916) and D'Arcy Thompson in *On Growth and Form* (1917), the project of the positive knowledge of form designated form as the slow process of adaptation to new function. As confused as matters become in the Alice stories, Alice never loses form and slides into a state of formlessness, though there is a hint of this when she admits to being afraid that her neck will grow beyond its capacity for growth (soon the example of the giraffe's neck would become paradigmatic within the new Darwinian morphology). At times she is afraid that she will burst, but her body apparently conforms to internal limits. Overwhelmingly morphology came to be concerned with these limits to development. 'At what point will I burst?' is a question which Alice consciously decides not to pursue, but which morphologists inspired by Darwin now set themselves to answer. The Darwinian morphology closely replicated Alice's concern with the limits of scale in formal transformation as it began to pose the question of the area between forms – how to understand it, how to represent it, how to manipulate it.

The Alice stories, then, occupy a transitional space between Linnaean and Darwinian morphologies. If Wonderland had made the world of the old logical morphology seem impossible, the new Darwinian morphology would make Wonderland seem doubly impossible. In Wonderland everything changes suddenly in accordance with the logic of language. In Darwin's morphology everything changes gradually, imperceptibly, the outcome of many random events ultimately selected out according to function. Ignorant of genetics, Darwin did not yet know why things changed gradually, but he firmly believed that evolution proceeds by slow and gradual stages. Once reconstructed, the complete sequence of organisms would be absolutely continuous throughout. There is no longer any place in Darwin's morphology for the catastrophic mutation of form. Monsters of form no longer have any place in a system which works out thoroughly the relationship of forms using the minima and maxima of calculus. Unusual, deviant, or monstrous forms can now be fixed on a vast index of change, a book of all changes. In Darwin's scheme, monsters either disappear forever or mutate themselves into a form which eventually becomes the norm. Change itself is stable and can be represented using what came to be known as 'topology.'

A topology is a reconstruction of the form of forms. The serial drawings showing apes gradually straightening their spines and breaking into a human gait were the first and most familiar topologies, but by the turn of the century topology had become abstract and multidimensional. It entailed the representation of what D'Arcy Thompson, the great elaborator of differential topology that came to characterize late-Victorian morphology, once called 'a difference of relative magnitudes, capable of tabulation by numbers and of complete expression by means of rectilinear coordinates.'[10] The ability to classify and manipulate all types of form was achieved only by giving up quantitative concepts of exact measurement such as employed by Linnaeus. Victorian morphology became largely a labor of guesswork, scraping the ground for a past for which little hard evidence existed, but which had necessarily to exist if Darwin was right. Every small shard of bone thus bore immense hermeneutic weight, and paleontologists came to be known for their abilities to piece together a whole animal from a single surviving bone.

The Darwinian morphology thus managed to open up a new era of positive knowledge without forsaking entirely the traditional assumption of the consonant whole. Darwinian morphology was equally a project of comprehensive knowledge, a theory of variation that nevertheless presupposed the inherent stability of biological processes. 'The form of the entire structure under investigation should be found to vary in a more or less uniform manner,' wrote Thompson, such that 'a comprehensive law of growth has pervaded the whole structure in its integrity, and that some more or less simple and recognizable system of forces has been in control.'[11] The emphasis on the control of the whole is striking. Though Thompson begs the question of what exactly is in control and how control is achieved and maintained, he assumes that control is unitary and comprehensive, exercised by a single 'system of forces.' The next section of this chapter will show how, in the late nineteenth century, this idea of a controlled whole derived from morphology began to take on an explicitly global, and finally imperial, coloration. The wholeness of the natural world became a figuration, in other words, for a united Empire. The assumption of the whole, which began almost as a matter of faith, thus ended as a central myth of imperial knowledge. In a great variety of ways the morphological idea of the earth as a single family tree acted as a new and vital counterpoint to the central myth of the British Empire, the myth traced in detail in the first chapter, the myth of the world as understandable by one conjoined imperial archive. A reading of Bram Stoker's *Dracula* will cast light on the process by which morphology became an imperial science of form that, beginning in the 1890s, began to imagine form coming apart at the seams, torn by the greatest threat that late-Victorian morphology saw to the whole, the specter of discontinuous mutation.

II

The new monsters were beings that had undergone, or were capable of undergoing, catastrophic mutations of form. They could pass from form to form, moving not one form at a time but skipping many forms in a single jump. In evolutionary theory, no form could finally remain fully separate from other forms. These monsters could do so. They introduced into morphology chasms of unbridgeable difference. Darwin had been actively concerned with trying to arrive at a comprehensive view of species as the product of gradual and small-scale mutation. In a great variety of ways, these beings were a new construction of monstrosity well suited to the blind spot in the Darwinian paradigm. They were what had just begun to be called 'mutants.'[12]

Certainly mutants were monstrous for the traditional reason that, even within the liberal guidelines for classification laid out by Darwin in *The Origin of Species*, they fell outside the domain of existing knowledge. But the mutant was something more than a being that eluded all existing structures of classification. A mutant is a being without a history. It has no past, no progenitors, no lineage, no putative position on a reconstructed time-line. A mutant cannot be understood topologically as a displacement and redistribution of a stable aggregate of formal features. The mutant eludes science's quantitative grasp of number and magnitude: it signals the presence of irrational, rather than rational, modes of changing form. The Darwinian world-view had encouraged a one-sided view of change that harmonized with other nineteenth-century views of the essential continuity of matter: the smoothly curving paths of planets around the sun, the continuously varying pressure of a gas as it heated and cooled, the quantitative increase of the sugar level in the bloodstream. The mutant entailed another kind of change, less suited to the assumption of a comprehensive knowledge regulating the behavior of all phenomena, a form of change like the abrupt bursting of a bubble or the discontinuous transition from ice at its melting point to water at its freezing point. This new mutantcy meant the sudden death of form. A mutant did not develop according to the calculus of variations, a form of forms; it was a form outside form.

This precise emphasis on discontinuous mutation led Bram Stoker to create a new and particularly imperial inflection of the myth of Dracula, lord and master of the Undead. Stoker erected a new mythology around an old myth because he made his Dracula into a single dense locus of all that the Darwinian world-view had found inexplicable. In particular, Stoker's Dracula forcibly undoes the assumptions of Darwinian morphology in the form of a creature capable of both *sudden* and *lasting* mutations of form. Stoker's vampire lurks in these two blind alleys of Darwinism. He is the origin of his own species, a human being suddenly transformed into the progenitor of a terrifying new species. And he is a being whom his opponents openly view as a mutant capable of the catastrophic mutation of form. He is an ideal invader of England for the simple reason that he cannot be understood according to the usual patterns of recurrence of form in nature. A mutant capable of singlehandedly and successfully crossing the boundary between species was entirely unknowable within the Darwinian frame of knowledge. Dracula represents a species having no gradual, composed origin. Little wonder that Stoker finds in his resuscitated vampire the material for a kind of Darwinian invasion novel. To the usual elements of the Dracula myth – the Transylvania setting, the wolves, the kisses of blood – he adds three elements: the sense of Dracula as a mutant; the association of Dracula with vegetable mould; and the shipment of the boxes of mould containing Dracula from the periphery of Europe to one of its centers, London. As a mutant, Count Dracula poses a direct threat to the order of things and, by extension, to the general order of an empire figured as knowable within a Darwinian frame of comprehensive morphological knowledge.

In Darwin the word 'mutation' had had an almost neutral connotation. All species originate by mutation, but mutation always remains safely subordinate to the functional criterion of natural selection. In Darwin the emphasis on adaptive function almost totally restricts the range of variant form. By the turn of the century, however, the Dutch plant breeder Hugo de Vries performed a number of botanical experiments with the evening primrose that proved decisively that new species could originate in a large, single jump. In the short space of one generation de Vries observed that the primrose changed leaf shape, incision, and color. In *The Mutation Theory* (1901–03) de Vries maintained that new species arose in one generation through the occurrence of large-scale variations, which he termed 'mutations.' Darwin had recognized the possibility of such a process in what he called 'sports' or 'monsters,' but he had rejected this mechanism as having little or no significant role in the production of species. The genius of Stoker's construction of Dracula is that, like de Vries, he realizes that the mutant is by no means a reproductive dead-end, that it has an immense potential for propagation. The narrative of *Dracula* takes on incredible suspense for the simple reason that Dracula must be stopped before he multiplies beyond the point where he can be extinguished. According to Van

Helsing, the scientist who scrupulously observes Dracula's habits in Stoker's novel, the most fearsome feature of the vampire is the speed at which he mutates. He learns quickly, changes forms quickly. This sense of large-scale jumps between forms gives a new sense to the old adage, 'The dead travel fast.'[13] Van Helsing comes right out and says that Dracula has been 'experimenting, and doing it well; and if it had not been that we had crossed his path he would be yet – he may be yet if we fail – the father or furtherer of a new order of beings, whose road must lead through Death, not Life' (302).

The consistent figure for death throughout Stoker's novel, and the one element with which Dracula is repeatedly associated, is vegetable mould. Previous Dracula stories had always likened the Vampire's lair to dust, but Stoker is very specific about his Dracula's preference for mould. When Jonathan Harker happens upon Dracula's sarcophagus in Transylvania he notices 'the odour of old earth newly turned' (47). The cargo Dracula ships to London consists of 'a number of great wooden boxes filled with mould' (80). This unlikely element was the subject of one of Darwin's most popular and practical books, *The Formation of Vegetable Mould through the Action of Worms* (1881). The relevant feature of vegetable mould is that, in Darwin's definition, it is matter that consists exclusively of the decaying residue of what was once living matter. Vegetable mould is matter in the median stage between life and death, matter that exists in a state of fertility. The role of worms is to fertilize the soil by turning over the earth like a plough, mixing the soil with leaves, twigs, the bones of dead animals, the harder parts of insects, the shells of land molluscs. Worms accelerate decay by subjecting the particles of earth 'to conditions eminently favourable for their decomposition and disintegration.'[14]

The representation of death as decomposition thus holds no mystery whatsoever for Darwin. Here as elsewhere Darwin sees decay as the primordial constituent of life on earth; the earth thrives on spent life, for the successive generations of life passing into death ensure the fertility of the topsoil. In the Victorian order of things the frightful thing about Dracula is not that he lives in a cemetery amidst dead things (the Victorians viewed cemeteries as familiar places) but that he lives in a purgatory of decay instead of just passing through it. Victorian popular culture was full of horror stories about the undecayed bodies of remarkable people, Paganinis and Lincolns whose bodies remained mysteriously immune to decay after death. In Stoker's novel the most terrifying moments come when his characters view the undecomposed bodies of vampires – when Jonathan Harker flees the sight of Dracula in his stone box, when the four men confront the dead Lucy in her tomb, when Van Helsing slays the three weird sisters in their Transylvanian crypt. Van Helsing goes so far as to say that even the sight of an undecomposed body is enough to cast a spell. The slight alteration the vampire makes in the Darwinian scheme, the one that makes him into an archetype of monstrosity within it, is that he does not complete the developmental process that forms the very precondition for life on earth. He dies without decaying, and flaunts his condition elementally by living in mould.

The new direction in which Stoker takes the Dracula myth also entails placing his Darwinian monster in a specifically imperial economy and making him pose a specifically imperial threat. Like so many other Victorian biologists, Darwin located the great incubators of mutation in the colonial world (even Wonderland, after all, is *under* England and contains colonial creatures like the hookah-smoking hookworm). Overwhelmingly the mutation tends to be represented as the revenge of the colonial world on the colonizer. Then as now, mutations at the periphery of the world – new forms, new creatures, new diseases – come back to haunt the world at its center. Transylvania was of course never a British colony, but Stoker makes his Dracula into the very type of the alienated colonial intellectual later analyzed with such acumen by Frantz Fanon.[15] In Stoker's narrative Dracula, a Magyar noble incensed at centuries of external domination that had reduced Transylvania to a Turkish colony, invades England from Transylvania. The basic movement of *Dracula* reverses the customary direction of colonization: in Stoker's novel the periphery attempts to colonize the center. Dracula brings with him not only an almost unlimited capacity for reproduction but also an association with the traditional carriers of the West's own ecological imperialism – rats, flies, mice, and vermin.[16] He proves a master at using Britain's imperial system of transport to his own advantage. He invades using the very shipping lines upon which Britain depended for receiving raw material from the colonial world. Most adeptly of all, he has mastered certain imperial practices of knowledge and power. He has worked at amassing a comprehensive knowledge of Britain, in Van Helsing's words, learning 'new social life; new environment of old ways, the politic, the law, the finance, the science, the habit of a new land and a new people who have come to be since he was' (321). In a sense he is pointing to a possibility that turn-of-the-century Britain could not bring itself to contemplate in the light of day: the possibility that the former colonist would emerge as the new immigrant, that Britain itself would emerge as a destination for immigrants from the colonial world. To prevent this from ever happening Stoker's characters adopt an unequivocal policy: 'We must sterilize all the imported earth' (274).

How could such a creature, a colonial creature capable of appropriating so many of the means of imperial domination to his own ends, ever be defeated? Dracula is defeated because, though he can control the transport of bodies and things, he cannot control the flow of information. At every point Stoker makes it crushingly clear that Dracula must be defeated through a mastery of the means of information. Dracula himself cannot move long distances; throughout the novel he is less a moving body than a point of inertia. Because Dracula must hire intermediaries to carry him from place to place, his movements can be traced through invoices, memoranda, and other documents. He uses transport without realizing that what he is confronting is a new kind of empire, an imperial archive already seen on view in Kipling's *Kim*, an empire in which all transport entails the production of data. His movements from place to place leaves traces in a language that his opponents can decipher, the language of information. 'Accurate note was made of the state of things' (79). It does not even occur to him to destroy documents that give his enemies some knowledge of him, like Jonathan Harker's journal. While Dracula moves in a state of stillness, waiting out the interval between arrival and departure, his opponents send and receive messages in the space of seconds using telegraphy. Distances mean nothing to Van Helsing and his crew of vampire-killers; they seem to traverse them in a flash. The spatial distance between central and peripheral zones makes way for temporal distance fixed by the imperial certainty of the train timetable. Even Lord Godalming's old-boy network joins the imperial archive, conveying messages rapidly from consulate to consulate in order to defeat Dracula. The dead travel fast but data travels faster.

In a great variety of ways, then, Stoker's narrative figures the defeat of a kind of colonial uprising. *Dracula* enacts the domination of a once-indomitable mutation by the imperial archive. The novel ends with an expedition to Transylvania in which the rebellious form is put to death. Like Lewis Carroll, Stoker takes care to represent indomitable form as despotic and absolutist, embodied in the form of Count Dracula, who 'spoke almost in the plural, like a king speaking' (28). Far from being represented as the wave of the future, the colonial uprising has been represented here, as it soon would be by the British all over their Empire, as the recrudescence of an obsolete form, absolutism. The monologues recorded by Jonathan Harker in his journal read like an inventory of the modes of control invented by the absolutist state; speaking of Transylvanian history, Dracula tells of the introduction of standing armies, a permanent bureaucracy, national taxation, a codified law, and the beginnings of a unified market.[17] Dracula is clearly a feudal lord who, over time, has come to think of himself as an absolutist monarch.

Van Helsing counters Dracula's universalism by slowly picking it apart. Like Auguste Comte, who sought to liberate politics from the influence of parties insisting on the divine right of kings by establishing a positive social science, Van Helsing counters Dracula's absolutism with a simple emphasis on the positive knowledge of form. Form for Van Helsing is not absolute and universal but particular and positive. He defeats Dracula by studying the functions of Dracula's form. He makes careful note of the vampire's habits and habitat. His manner of investigation is a model of experimental method, and he refuses to explain to the others that the mysterious occurrences in the novel have been caused by a supernatural phenomenon until he can supply them with sufficient proof. Even though he is dealing with vampires, Van Helsing preserves all the assumptions of the positive knowledge of form, maintaining the presumed integrity of the world though what can be called an imperialism of particulars. In *Dracula* 'the habit of entering accurately' (36) along with 'power of combination' (238) ensure the reach of the Empire. At stake throughout the novel are the methods and procedures for controlling the imperial whole, and the primary vehicle for the control of the whole, a whole that can now comprise the irrational as well as the rational, is the procedure of positive knowledge.

Despite the defeat of Dracula by a smoothly functioning imperial archive, however, the novel has a prospective and unmistakably postcolonial character, for in it the boundaries of Empire have contracted. The boundaries of Empire have fallen back from Africa and India to an obscure danger zone at the edge of Europe. Contrary to Kipling, the novel begins at the place where East and West actually meet. At Budapest, Harker has the impression that 'we were leaving the West and entering the East,' entering 'one of the wildest and least known portions of Europe' (1). He represents the Balkan region using the stock figures of orientalism: the trains run late as 'in China,' the people remind him of 'some old Oriental band of brigands,' all in all the region is 'the centre of some sort of imaginative whirlpool' in which is gathered 'every known superstition in the world' (2–3). Throughout the nineteenth century the Balkans were like a trip wire waiting to be crossed. The famous 'Eastern Question' came into being to address the fall of the Ottoman and Persian empires and the emergence of superpower rivalry among successor states in the region.[18] The narrative of *Dracula* runs along the retaining wall that separated imperial Europe from the imagined deluge of the colonial world, but it also points to the source of a very real catastrophe. The liminal zone of the Balkans, marked off by Stoker as the home of vampires, the site of mutation and locus of monstrosity, is the very place where the First World War began, the very place where the great colonial empires of the late nineteenth century began to end.

For nearly one hundred years the myth of Dracula has fed off this precise tension between continuous and discontinuous mutation, between an imperial order figured as continuous and a colonial disorder figured as formal discontinuity. In Stoker's novel the threat of discontinuity turns out at last to be manageable. Dracula is defeated, but only just. The triumph of the forces of Darwinian order over the forces of mutant disorder requires a last-minute high-speed chase in which the outcome is uncertain until the very last page. After two debilitating world wars it would no longer be possible to imagine the defeat of such a prodigy of mutation spawned in the colonial world. As a myth of knowledge the mutation would rise again in the imagination of postcolonial

Britain. The last section of this chapter will show how the mutation took its place as a primary myth of decolonization, a myth of a force out of Africa, beyond the range of understanding, unstoppable, a myth of the world transformed into a latticework of crystal.

III

In the science of form, the ancient distinction between *forma* and *materia* remained in force well into the twentieth century. Aristotle had held that there could be form without matter, though no matter without form. As late as the 1940s Joseph Needham was still criticizing morphologists for devoting themselves to the study of living form 'without much consideration of the matter with which it is indissolubly connected.'[19] The classic texts of morphology do focus almost exclusively on the stately progress from form to form. Whether they deal with continuous or discontinuous change, the morphologists all end up by positing a structural stability in which forms join at specific junctions to compose the pattern of a whole. In *On Growth and Form*, D'Arcy Thompson devotes almost no space to the particular forces that cause forms to change. Nor does the scientist in *Dracula* take any interest in the material composition of his monster of mutation; Dracula exists for Van Helsing not as a chemical substance but as a continuum of changing forms. Form in morphology is almost entirely a matter of aesthetics, and the assumption joining all morphological thought is that all forms must turn out in the end to be beautiful, however violently they may at first jar the conventions of perception (even vampires appear at beautiful ease in their final moment of destruction). Over time the science of form has supplied a variety of aestheticisms with a basic lexicon of beauty, the vocabulary of ideal design, even as it extended the domain of the aesthetic to include new shapes of life and death.[20]

Viewed within this tradition of morphological interpretation, J.G. Ballard's *The Crystal World* (1966) performs an important reversal. In Ballard's novel the traditional emphasis on the form of material gives way, temporarily at least, to a new emphasis on the material of form. Ballard's novel turns on the formal behavior of a specific material in a specific place, an unknown crystalline substance that first appears in the Republic of Cameroon on the coast of central Africa. *The Crystal World* examines the genesis of a new form and probes its underlying structural stability as matter. The crystals grow with predictable regularity, producing hallucinatory distortions and blurring the very lines that indicate form. This new material calls into question the unities of formal evolution as understood by Victorian morphology. It attacks the very place where forms multiply in profligate number, destroying an immensely variegated tropical ecosystem like one of those described by Darwin during his *Beagle* voyage. Victorian biology had marked off Africa as a place where new forms originate. In some respects Ballard's novel ought to be considered a companion piece to Joseph Needham's classic *Biochemistry and Morphogenesis* (1942), for in it Ballard marks off Africa as the continent where a new kind of matter is responsible for dictating a new configuration of form.

Ballard gives a specific postcolonial inflection to this new twentieth-century morphology of matter. For Ballard formal unity is quite simply no longer tenable as a metaphor for empire. In *The Crystal World* the unity of form is drastically modified by the introduction of a new kind of matter. Slowly expanding forces come out of Africa and threaten to take over the world, and everyone is powerless to stop them. In part this transformation of the world into a new kind of matter can be understood as a way of figuring the vast expansion of the mineral resource base of imperial Europe (even the dissolution of the colonial empires took place amidst a vast increase in the minerals processed for export from the colonies to Europe). But the expansion of the crystal forest can be better understood as a myth of decolonization without agency. Between 1960 and 1966 twelve former British colonies had become independent African nations (Cameroon had broken with France in 1960). The novel begins amidst the political debris of decolonization, and from page to page the political control of Cameroon simply erodes. The local authorities call in the army and impose a censorship around the affected zone, but Ballard makes it clear that nobody is responsible for what is happening. Playing off the convention of science fiction according to which new developments in the colonial world are assumed to originate in outer space, Ballard takes care to make the origins of the crystal form extraplanetary and obscure. The earth is predominantly crystalline, but this threatening new African crystal comes from outer space. The result is an originless species of matter that weaves a layered structure of exquisitely equilibrated forms across equatorial Africa.

The sense of the imperial whole, then, does not entirely disappear from *The Crystal World*. Instead, one kind of whole succeeds another. Mutations, which Bram Stoker had figured as a threat to the unity of empire, now possess a postcolonial integrity all their own. The formerly imperial whole now assumes a discontinuous and unstable form – broken, like the African continent itself, into separate nations, each with its own line of development. Ballard is fascinated by the politics of the fractured regularity of crystal growth. Crystals grow until something gets in their way, at which point they break into points and planes of disorder.[21] Either the crystal is riddled with interstitial impurities or it bumps up against an adjacent crystal and comes to an end. The crystal is a paradigm of national growth in a postcolonial world, where nations are little wholes, self-generating systems that develop according to their own inner logic, multiplying and finally colliding. If the imperial aspirations of the nineteenth century were symbolically encapsulated in the idea of morphological lineage in which all parts formed an imperial whole, the various discrete nationalisms of twentieth-century life find representation in the idea of the discontinuous development characterized by sharp breaks, irruptions and interruptions. The empire had formerly seemed to unfold as one Darwinian world; the nations now seem to join together, Ballard perceives, as modular elements of a crystal world.

A crystal does not at first seem like a likely candidate for monstrosity. In the early modern period, monsters were fabulous beings compounded of elements from human and animal forms. The eighteenth century saw monsters as beings falling outside the logic of taxonomical groupings, while in the nineteenth century, the only monsters allowable were weak, marginal beings, which Darwin called 'sports,' beings having only a marginal chance of survival due to structural defects or deformities. In each period monsters offered paradigms of contact with alterity, seeing the other respectively as an animal, a category, an inferior. Today the monster no longer represents a human, or even a remotely human, alterity. The peoples of the earth are mostly well known, so we have relegated monstrosity not merely to outer space, as in science fiction, where monsters tend to assume their most traditional forms, but also, and more tellingly, to anything scientifically unknown. The figure of Dracula remains popular in modern retellings because he conforms to both molds; he is an alien in the twin senses of the word, both a foreigner invading England and a member of a very different species falling outside the domain of conventional scientific knowledge, a being also, then as now, associated with plague and incurable disease. Today, when the unknown is very frequently a statistical construction, the monster is a fluke. Indeed the one force most capable of raising again the specter of monstrosity is the discovery of a rare statistical entity, an entity falling outside the norms of probabilistic distribution.[22] *The Crystal World* is full of images of all sorts of prodigies of improbability – random variations, strange viruses, rare diseases, new kinds of matter. What happens when scientific knowledge confronts the improbable? The improbable approaches the outermost limits of positive knowledge; beyond the frontier knowledge becomes myth, a matter of aesthetics. The first part of the novel turns on Dr Sanders's investigation of the material of this new crystal form. Like all the other characters in the novel, he gives up trying to understand the material but realizes that he is still capable of appreciating its form. Approaching the edge of statistical knowledge, he stops trying to understand the material of the crystal's form and begins, like a Victorian morphologist, to appreciate the form of the crystal's material. Coming up against the sheer unknowability of the material of a new form, Sanders shows just how easy it is to return to the traditional morphological strategy of constructing an explicitly aesthetic valuation of the form of an unknown material. Ballard, however, offers a new twist, for in his novel the monstrous, far from being an ugly portent, offers entry into the realm of the beautiful.

The only form of evaluation that finally makes any sense at all of the form of the new crystal matter is aesthetic valuation. At different points in the novel, Ballard's characters attempt to comprehend the crystal growth by observing its mechanical, chemical, and gravitational tendencies. They observe that leather repels it, water dissolves it, gravity obstructs its vertical movement. The most remarkable feature of the crystal, however, is the ease with which everyone in the novel accepts it. The world's nations do not massively mobilize their technological resources to face this threat to life on the planet.

Rather, people lose themselves in contemplating a new conception of life, a new unity of matter and form. In the eighteenth century Goethe had sought to discover what he called the *Urpflantze*, the one plant that would typify all of the different kinds of plant life. For most of his life Goethe expected to know it at once if he came upon it, for the archetypal plant would be 'the strangest growth the world has ever seen.'[23] In Ballard's novel the strange archetypal plant is a mineral that strives to fulfill an ideal aesthetic design, and most of Ballard's characters respond by acting as if, somehow, somewhere, they had seen the form before. The recognition of the beauty of the crystal growth occupies most of the novel as character after character falls rapt before the crystals, speaking in explicitly aesthetic terms of a new kind of integrity and of a heightened sense of affinity with the matter of a new form.

This aestheticization of alterity embodied as crystal is the central symbolic strategy of the novel, and it points to a powerful process of postcolonial semiosis. In *The Crystal World* the world's authorities can do absolutely nothing to stop the crystals from spreading across Africa or, for that matter, from travelling across the surface of the earth. But they can and do construct them as purely aesthetic artifacts. Ballard's characters feel 'less concerned to find a so-called scientific explanation for the phenomenon' and more concerned to see how 'the beauty of the spectacle had turned the keys of memory.'[24] To represent the crystals Ballard does not draw on the arcane language of modern crystallography to introduce a new construction of the sublime. The old sublime still serves very well here, performing its traditional cultural work as Ballard explicitly summons the imagery of wave after wave of Western aesthetic valuation to make the strange familiar. Ballard's imagery has an almost canonical solidity. Images evoking the form of the new crystal material appear from medieval friezes, quattrocento Italian painting, Renaissance sculpture, Baroque architecture, Romantic poetry, Pre-Raphaelite painting. His characters can often sound like Ruskin in Venice. At no point in the novel does the crystal form make an appearance outside of its museum-case of aesthetic valuation. What finally contains the crystal form is very simply the certainty that it can and will be susceptible to representation using the received repertoire of aesthetic tropes.

The crystal 'world' of central Africa thus exists primarily as a sequence of images frozen in highly artificial aesthetic frames. The world as crystal does not compose itself into one single picture; rather, there are many successive pictures, and the total effect is explicitly cinematic. 'The long arc of trees hanging over the water seemed to drip and glitter with myriads of prisms, the trunks and branches sheathed by bars of yellow and carmine light that bled away across the surface of the water, as if the whole scene were being reproduced by some over-active Technicolor process' (76). The scenes in the novel do not reveal an essentially synchronic strategy for containing the world within the frame of a single world picture – the composed world, say, of a nineteenth-century colonial exhibition. They rather reveal a diachronic strategy of containment in which the alien crystal form is represented not singly but serially. The world cannot be packed into one single picture, but the certainty that it can be represented nevertheless has continued undiminished and results in the aesthetic raptures with which the novel's characters view even the most terrifying manifestations of material and formal alterity. In Britain the conditions of a positive knowledge had long acted to foreshorten the field of representation. by implication, only the knowable could be represented. In Ballard's novel the unknown may turn out at last to be unknowable, but even in its unknowability it remains fully susceptible to the conditions of containment imposed by the aesthetic means of Western representation.

Even the end of the world appears primarily as an aesthetic event that asserts the existence of the world as a single entity over which Western representation still presides. A crystal world is a ruined world full of the 'derelict monuments' (167) of the Western past. The first chapter of this book has shown that the idea of the world as a single geography was a product of the colonial empires of the late nineteenth century. The 'world' was never more than a normative concept for imagining the implementation of empire.[25] Similarly the 'end of the world' was never more than a way of imagining the end of empire. The world ends as a whole. In The Crystal World the world is also united only by its destruction. This destruction is of a limited and partial kind, however, for the crystal apocalypse does not so much annihilate the world as transform its separate nations into little identical units of crystal. At the end of the novel the crystal is a paradigm of fractured national growth tending toward a diffuse new dominion. Frozen in crystal, the world is once again an empire of sorts. Unitary and dominating, the crystal form perpetrates a likeness that takes final precedence over the differences among nations. The tensions between the nations of the world disappear as they await final union. The crystal world must be seen as proposing a quintessentially postcolonial image: the image of an empire without colonies, an empire in which there are no colonies, an empire that manages to persist without holding colonies, an empire like Britain's today, an empire in which one of the world's largest navies exists primarily to keep up the appearance of empire.

The final metamorphosis in Ballard's novel reminds us that, even today, morphology remains an archive of imperial knowledge. In many respects the science of form epitomizes the ideological relation between archive and empire: the sciences of empire all become pseudo-sciences in their imperial fields of application. All knowledge becomes marginal at the margins. The methods, means, and procedures for constructing a positive knowledge of the world at its European center become the material for constructing a mythology of the world at its colonial periphery. This process can often be pushed so far that knowledge lapses completely into myth, as when the means of a traditional physiognomy became the tools of a racist phrenology. The effort to construct a total knowledge of the world captures the imagination, but ultimately it fails. The failure of morphology to encompass the world as one has been protracted, and even today morphology survives as marginal science like René Thom's 'catastrophe theory' or the aesthetic constructions of chaotic dynamics.[26] It remains one of the last great enduring aestheticisms of the late nineteenth century.

In the late nineteenth century the project of morphology had become a myth of knowledge not only because it equipped scientists with a new way of eliminating the monstrous and provided aestheticians with a new way of constructing the beautiful, but also and much more importantly because it provided imaginative access to a field of knowledge coextensive with the Empire itself. Morphology was imperial science, and it joined political economy and physics in making a myth of Empire as a coherent imperium of Western knowledges. Over the past one hundred years morphology has slowly slipped from prominence as Britain experimented with other ways of constructing knowledge that provided a more comprehensive access to the epistemological field of its Empire. Joseph Needham was well aware of the kind of knowledge that had succeeded morphology in its effort to figure empire as a formal totality. 'Form is not the perquisite of the morphologist,' he wrote in 1942. 'It exists as the essential characteristic of the whole realm of organic chemistry, and cannot be excluded either from "inorganic" chemistry or nuclear physics. But at that level it blends without distinction into order as such, and hence we should do well to give up all the arguments about form and matter, replacing them by two factors more in accordance with what we now know of the universe, that is to say, Organization and Energy.'[27] This index of lower and higher levels of organization throughout the world was called 'entropy.'

THREE

ARCHIVE AND ENTROPY

The last quarter of the nineteenth century saw the formation and consolidation of an imagined organon of global knowledge and power. The idea of the imperial archive was an early version of today's fantasies of a world unified by information. Today it is easy to see that, all by itself, information cannot possibly possess all the powers attributed to it. Like power, information does not exist in a vacuum. It has to be made and used. Data has no inherent function and can just as easily lend itself to open societies as closed ones. The first two chapters of this book have shown how the late-nineteenth-century state took on many of the attributes of the archive. Though the archive threatened at times to overwhelm the state with a mountain of documents, more often the state began to imagine that it could perform feats of magic with knowledge, doing a lot more than merely acting as its curator. A variety of narratives succeeded in transforming the uncontrolled accumulation of knowledge into a fantasy of a controlled flow of information to and from the state. This system was myth before it became something like fact, and as the first chapter has shown, the combination of positivist and mythical material in texts such as Rudyard Kipling's *Kim* (1901) provides an exemplary instance of the way in which the conditions and possibility of total knowledge began as mythical constructions but ended as the vast imagined community of the state.[1] In the late nineteenth century, a new construction of mythical state control, a new Leviathan, had developed to make some sense out of all the knowledge being gathered by the British Empire. Hobbes had once imagined the vast unity of the state as 'the finall Cause, End, or Designe of Men,' and in *Leviathan* (1651) he makes the case that the state exists for the sake of society, which would disintegrate without

73

it.[2] The nineteenth century had seen a vast extension of state control over every area of life. Much Victorian thought participated in seeing the state as central to human life, and more, in imagining a kind of complete documentary knowledge of human life that would exist solely for the state. The thread uniting the thought of Bentham and Mill with the thought of Russell and Keynes and C.P. Snow was the idea that knowledge is inconceivable without the state: that the question of the state is a question of knowledge, especially scientific knowledge; that the classing of knowledge must be underwritten and directed by the state in its various capacities; that all epistemology became and must remain state epistemology in an economy of controlled information.

The idea of a perfectly balanced economy of information always verged on ideology, and throughout the nineteenth century Britain tended to regard the information it collected as belonging to an extended British public sphere. The state itself was basically viewed as the most visible manifestation of the public sphere, 'the sphere of private people come together as a public,' and as shown, the blueprint for the modern state originated not in moribund public institutions like the monarchy but in private-turned-public institutions like the museum.[3] But whereas in the eighteenth century the proponents of the public sphere had argued that the integrity of the channels of internal communication was essential to the welfare of society, the clerisy of the imperial archive now perceived that the integrity of the channels of external communication was essential to the welfare of the Empire. The people who ran the knowledge-producing institutions of Victorian England considered the archive they had fashioned as a sort of vast railway switch yard capable of being controlled by the right signals and switches, if only they could be found. The new Leviathan didn't swallow information but spewed it out in a steady stream of small bits of paper, brief coded messages, timetables, telegraph codes, and red tape.

But it must be remembered that a lot of information never got where it was going. In South Africa Boer guerrillas learned to cut telegraph cables. A lot of books dropped into the bottomless pit of the British Museum basement. The post office jostled dead letters. Journalists mangled the news as they saw fit. Dickens's Circumlocution Office is a lasting testimony to the view that there was now too much knowledge for knowledge to have a center. And yet, despite these difficulties, texts like *Kim* and *Dracula* routinely represent information passing through a noiseless environment without attrition. Among the spies in the India Survey or Van Helsing's crew of vampire-hunters, information seems to pass with little expense or loss of energy. The ideal, preserved despite much evidence to the contrary, was of a global space of Empire maximally purged of blockage, and the best spaces of all, according to Alfred Thayer Mahan, the great Victorian theorist of the sea, were those approximating the emptiness of the sea, which he considered 'free of obstructions.'[4]

This confidence in the communicational transparency of knowledge had been inherited from the Victorian positivists. Awareness of the problem of interference in transmitting knowledge increased markedly in the 1860s and 1870s just as the possibility of positive knowledge began to be perceived as eroding.[5] Thanks to certain striking developments in British thermodynamics, the field that replaced the hydrodynamics of the eighteenth century, this theory of information loss usually took on a scientific coloration. In British physics, the problem of positive knowledge within information systems received such extensive consideration that today its central figures, William Thomson (later Lord Kelvin) and James Clerk Maxwell, occupy key positions in the history of cybernetics. Beginning in the 1860s, physicists studied the problem of information loss using a variety of models. The measure of information loss came to be called 'entropy,' a term first proposed by Rudolf Clausius in 1865 as an index of the loss of information. The Victorians devised entropy as a measure of information, and it became the most important epistemological index of the century and, arguably, the nineteenth century's most vital link to our own world. It appeared in key texts of applied mathematics and macroeconomics. By the turn of the century many of the empire's communications glitches had been defined as examples of entropy, or the tendency of matter to move from an organized to a disorganized state. Victorian theorists of entropy began the recognizably modern work of trying to figure out how to organize information so as to cope with chance events and evade disorganization. This involved reorienting the idea of the archive – Britain's projected imperial domain of comprehensive knowledge – around the axis of entropy.

This chapter looks at how, in the late nineteenth century, the problem of the disorganization of knowledge came to replace the problem of the organization of knowledge. Our idea of information still has something about it of the frustration the Victorians felt at watching all their knowledges fly apart. Information is knowledge fractured into bits and pieces that can be moved around easily but never really assembled successfully into an integrated whole. The fact that information could be moved quickly did not necessarily mean that it could be moved from place to place without attrition. People began to see that though large amounts of information could now be sent from place to place, it was not the quantity of the information sent but the quality of the information received that counted. The concept of entropy came into being precisely because the possibility of positive knowledge was beginning to be eclipsed by an explosion of too much positive knowledge. Information was the name given to this knowledge that came from everywhere and ended nowhere. Information was archival without belonging to an archive, vast but not total, extensive but not complete. Information was positive knowledge that refused to become comprehensive. Information meant knowledge without the central structuring agency of an archive, or a totalizing metastable structure for knowledge. The Victorian information explosion threatened the sense that human understanding could ever achieve mastery over knowledge. Soon the sense of entropy as basic to information eroded the belief, still widespread, that not even an expanded state, let alone an expanded human consciousness, could handle all of it.

The Victorian state had long maintained an informal but searching interest in those who sought to develop new technologies for extending control over knowledge. Since the parliamentary hearings on the conditions and constitution of the British Museum in the 1840s, the state had attempted to force a criterion of performance on Britain's informal state institutions of knowledge. In the 1860s the concept of entropy became the basic tool for measuring the performance of information systems, and it proved to be a major impetus to state control over knowledge. Even the first theorists of entropy saw its use in figuring out why information was so hard to contain and control. By the beginning of the twentieth century thermodynamics had developed into a theory of communication whose exponents introduced the now familiar concepts of noise and redundancy. This chapter follows the series of transformations by which British information theorists confronted the problem of entropic disorganization, creating new modes of counter-organization that ultimately became the basis for making the state into the central information-gathering apparatus of modern life. The first part of the chapter deals with a series of classic thermodynamic texts written in the 1870s by James Clerk Maxwell. The second part is a reading of H.G. Wells's *Tono-Bungay* (1909), a novel which explicitly links an increase in imperial entropy with the consolidation of the modern state. The third examines the epistemology of entropy in the militarized London of Thomas Pynchon's *Gravity's Rainbow* (1973). Taken together, these texts reconstruct the process by which entropy, the measure of disorganization, became and remained a central organizational function of the imperial archive.

I

One of the first unified field theories in history was a theory of heat. In the mid-nineteenth century a number of scientists formulated a joint theory of energy, force, and matter that tried to provide a representation of the transmission of heat through space. Classical mechanics, though comprehensive enough to attempt an explanation of what Newton called 'the system of the world,' had not really succeeded in constructing an explanation of the mechanism by which heat was propagated. In his *Principia* (1686), Newton generally refrained from discussing the nature of matter, focusing his argument instead on solid mechanics and, to a lesser degree, fluid mechanics. Seventeenth-century physics was overwhelmingly concerned with gravitation and the mechanics of weights, while eighteenth-century physics extended the domain of investigation to include hydrodynamics and the mechanics of fluids. The mechanical representation of bodies in motion almost never considered fundamental questions about the nature of heat, which tended to be represented either as a solid (the ether) or as a fluid (the imponderable fluid) phenomenon. Whatever the details, the general effort was to derive a theory of heat from a mechanical view of nature that saw matter in motion as the basis of all physical phenomena. Though in theory the laws of mechanical motion had been designed as a comprehensive set of demonstrable propositions deduced from a small number of postulates, in practice they left the field of physical knowledge open and incomplete. Newton's mechanics of the individual projectile, a phenomenology of the path of the line linking point with point, had created a ballistic world picture in which intervening objects took the form of obstacles. But it ignored the various thermal phenomena pervading space and preventing the easy transfer of bodies in motion. In the nineteenth century, the study of these mediating forces led to a reconsideration of the epistemology of heat and to a theory of ambient space which included not only a new explanation of the nature of motion (the statistical flux of Brownian motion) but also a theory devised to account for the impact of differences of temperature on motion. The century that deployed the steam engine and developed the internal combustion engine also created a unified field theory of heat as entropy.[6]

This concern with impediments to motion was new. Since the seventeenth century, physical science had produced a mechanical representation of the world which, as part of Newton's system of the world, posited the mechanical transmission of bodies in motion. In this mechanistic epistemology all motion was locomotion; all motion replicated the motion of the earth and complied exactly with its force, gravity; and all motion tended to be equated with the movement of large bodies (planets and projectiles) rather than with the movement of small ones (molecules and particulate matter). As proposed by James Clerk Maxwell in 1854, the theory of the unified field addressed not only the movement of bodies but also the conditions, thermal and electromagnetic, separating them.[7] In field theory the conditions separating bodies were at least as important as the bodies themselves. More than anything else, field theory was a theory of the phenomena obstructing the unmediated movement of bodies through space. The mechanistic epistemology had always emphasized the regularity of individual bodies in motion: a movable body was a knowable body, as numerous ballistics manuals such as Crantz's *Exterior Ballistics* (1861) attested. Much of Victorian science, rather, came to be concerned with the irregularity of bodies in motion and, more generally, with the unknowability of movement itself. Though couched in mechanical terms, the discovery in

1826 of Brownian motion opened up the possibility that a mechanical system may also be irregular; that bodies in motion drift from order to disorder; that all movement displays an irreversible tendency toward bias.

The nineteenth-century effort to reconcile mechanistic epistemology with the theory of heat was called thermodynamics, or the study of heat (then called 'thermotics') joined to the study of motion (then called 'dynamics'). Like Newton, Thomson and Maxwell assumed that heat consists of the motions of particles of bodies, and they sought to formulate thermodynamics as an extension of the mechanistic epistemology. But their project of unifying mechanical and thermal processes had unintended consequences. The questioning of heat opened the way for a new epistemological field in which the knowledge of heat became the template for many other kinds of knowledge. For the foregrounding of heat – and with it the concepts of energy, force, and matter – began a massive process of deconstruction within Victorian science that resulted in the dismantling of the mechanical world-view. Thomson and Maxwell drove a wedge between mechanical and thermal phenomena and laid the groundwork for the statistical mechanics of Ludwig Boltzmann. Boltzmann was the last Casaubon of science, the last major scientific thinker to attempt to construct a comprehensive mechanical model encompassing alike solid, liquid and gaseous phenomena; like Thomson he believed in the possibility of a unified and systematic mechanical model. It took many years before thermodynamics went beyond Thomson's declaration that the construction of a mechanical model of a phenomenon was the criterion of the intelligibility of that phenomenon; not until the 1920s did Planck assert that all mechanical models were little better than orreries.[8] Nevertheless, in a great variety of ways Victorian thermodynamics signalled a new direction in epistemology by positing the unknowability of the movement of particular bodies. For in the thermodynamics of James Clerk Maxwell, movement became no longer a certainty but a probability.

The probabilistic character of movement forms a central line of investigation in the classic text of Victorian thermodynamics, James Clerk Maxwell's *Theory of Heat* (1872). Based on the assumption that heat issues from motion, this text comprises an anatomy of the 'statistical knowledge of bodies.'[9] By statistical knowledge Maxwell means a very specific kind of knowledge, a knowledge neither particular nor general. At no point does he try, as Newton did, to observe or define the behavior of particular molecules. Nor does he attempt, as the eighteenth-century taxonomists did, to formulate general rules regulating the behavior of each and every molecule. His concern is rather with knowledge as a sort of composite portrait compiled from existing sets of photographs superimposed over one another. The image produced represents neither a known particular quality (an individual mark like a mole) nor a known general quality (a common feature like a Roman nose). This is knowledge as a synthetic mean, knowledge that Maxwell explicitly terms 'statistical information,' a term for which the shorter 'information' soon sufficed. For Victorian sociologists like Henry Mayhew and William Farr, information had meant atomized facts organized into highly individual and not necessarily representative taxonomies. For Victorian biologists like Darwin and Louis Agassiz, information still meant large and binding structures of classification.[10] Maxwell was one of the first to use the word in its modern sense of an entity that lacks both generality and particularity. The inflection he gave the term proved to be very influential: for Maxwell, information is knowledge composed to form a single space, at once homogeneous and heterogeneous, at the joint loss of its generality and its particularity. The model of all knowledge has become not positive but probable knowledge.

The particular index of the probable knowledge of molecular motion within Victorian thermodynamics was called entropy. Entropy was from the start primarily an index of information. Following Rudolf Clausius, Maxwell used the concept of entropy as an index of the statistical knowledge of bodies. Strictly speaking, in Clausius's original 1865 definition, entropy is no more than a measure of the speed at which bodies move from order to disorder in conformity with the Second Law of Thermodynamics, the inexorable tendency of the universe, and any closed system in it, to slide toward a state of increasing disorder. This law does not mandate, as has often been wrongly supposed, the impossibility of ordered structures.[11] Nor does it presuppose a Manichean dialectic in which the forces of order confront the forces of chaos. For, according to the Second Law, disorder is not the negation of order. Disorder, rather, is the ordinal condition of all movement, the result of the automatic random mixing of molecules. The central presupposition of Victorian thermodynamics is that even though disorder has not been induced, and even though it cannot be predicted in any precise way, it can be measured using the index of entropy. The first theorists of entropy simply accepted that the particulars of any knowledge have a somewhat random and arbitrary character. To measure energy transmitted and transformed, they began not by assuming order but by assuming disorder, and worked consistently from the assumption that their knowledge was approximate at best, and far more likely to fall apart than to come together.[12]

Much of Maxwell's *Theory of Heat* deals with the problem of the degree to which the transmission of heat entails the entropic transformation of matter, or more simply, the degree to which all work requires heat. To a later edition of the text he added a passage that proved to be the most famous riddle of the nineteenth century, the riddle of Maxwell's demon. The Maxwell demon is a vision of thermodynamics upside down, a parable of a situation in which a hot body could take heat from a colder body without performing external work on the system, thus violating the Second Law of Thermodynamics (today this dream goes by the name of 'cold fusion'). Maxwell considered a gas in a vessel divided into two sections, A and B, by a diaphragm. Relatively speaking, A was hot and B was cold. But because of Maxwell's own velocity distribution law, he assumed that both sectors would have a range of velocities of all magnitudes; A could be called hot only because it had a higher average kinetic energy than B. Maxwell then imagined a 'finite being' who could observe the motions and velocities of the individual gas molecules. This being would open and close a hole in the diaphragm, selecting the molecules so that faster molecules in the cold side would pass into the hot side, while slower molecules from the hot side would pass into the cold side. The result of this process would be that 'the energy in A is increased and that in B is diminished; that is, the hot system has got hotter and the cold colder and yet no work has been done, only the intelligence of a very observant and neat-fingered being has been employed.'[13]

The Maxwell demon was the first propriocepter, the first sensory receptor for receiving and processing information. The reason the demon posed a conundrum to Victorian thermodynamics is that Maxwell and his contemporaries persisted in imagining the demon as a valve in an engine that could produce heat without the expenditure of work. What they did not understand, however, was that the demon was less a valve than an electric eye that could perform advanced functions of surveillance without using electricity, a fully automated control tower that required no external monitoring or source of power, a kind of panoptic perpetual-motion machine. In Maxwell's parable, the sense of sight provides the means for controlling entropy without itself being subject to the entropic process. The demon needs to see the various molecules in order to distinguish their velocities. Here Maxwell presupposes that the demon commands a view of a Cartesian field of uniform and unimpeded visibility. No fluctuation such as radiation interferes with the visual field, and the light that strikes the demon's eye does not share in the entropic properties of mechanical motion itself. Equipped with an ideal sight machine, Maxwell finally presupposed that the demon was capable of achieving a complete and exact definition of the given initial state of its system – a complete positive knowledge which even Comte regarded as an impossibility. In Borges's parable of an emperor who commissions a perfectly accurate map of his empire, the project leads the country to ruin because the entire population devotes all its energy to cartography.[14] In the parable of the demon, Maxwell assumes the existence of such a map, for the demon's perfect control over its system, a control without catastrophe, issues from perfect knowledge of the system's variables, and the result is comprehensive knowledge, albeit on a very small scale.

The Maxwell demon took up a central position in late Victorian culture because it figured an absolutely neutral space of transmission. It further constructed a situation in which information obtained across this space cost absolutely nothing (the demon is somehow capable of furnishing its own power source). The demon has a perfect signal-to-noise ratio. In the demon's system energy can be transformed, and information transmitted, without loss or waste. The demon does not merely minimize entropy: it gives something for nothing by countering entropy through feedback. More than anything else, the demon is a paralogy of control through mechanical observation, and in his parable Maxwell conforms to classical mechanics even as he posits a situation that violates the Second Law of Thermodynamics. The crucial point here is that the thermal control of the vessels devolves on the successful manipulation of a very small percentage of the molecules contained within them. Maxwell wanted to show that a 'mechanism' could 'guide and control' a system by actually guiding and controlling only a small part of it (140). And the small part necessary to systemic control need only be seen to be susceptible to control. He wanted to show, in other words, that entropy could somehow be controlled without the catastrophic consequences envisioned by Borges. The global direction of entropy could be countered locally if controlled mechanically by and through the magical visual agency – a transcendental and universal eye – of what Maxwell persists in calling a 'finite being.'

The Maxwell demon quickly became one of the most overdetermined constructions in Victorian thought. The reception accorded the Maxwell demon within scientific circles pales beside the many optimistic assessments, within Victorian culture at large, of the potential of thermodynamics for controlling entropy through technological means. It is worth remembering here that Victorian thermodynamics regarded the slightest tampering with any closed system as tantamount to catastrophe. Nineteenth-century scientists were the first to regard catastrophes as what René Thom calls 'discontinuities of the environment' issuing from a series of human and technological interventions.[15] In this view any disturbance of a metastable system is tantamount to disaster. The problem of the demon, rather, presupposes the structural stability of the entropic process. Later in his life, in his *Treatise on Electromagnetism* (1878), Maxwell was to take an interest in the catastrophic effects that local and unpredictable shock waves had on electromagnetic fields. But he initially regarded the entropic process as stable and predictable enough (statistical knowledge, after all, presupposes statistical knowability) to make it susceptible to control by an entity like the demon. It was this stability that led him to posit, in a striking and memorable way, the use-value of entropy within the economic process of mid-Victorian capitalism.

Victorian views of the entropic process almost always see it as a component of a controlled economy, a version of capitalism in which the disorder of the market has been brought to order by some form of state intervention. A link had always existed between classical mechanics and classical economics, both of which had posited mechanistic systems of the world in which matter in motion (or commodities in exchange) had a privileged status. Just as the general laws of dynamics treated the interaction of solid, liquid and gaseous bodies as forms of motion, the principle of the wealth of nations saw the interaction of production, distribution, and consumption as the production of wealth through the motion of circulation. In the nineteenth century, however, the new science of thermodynamics did not simply bear a close resemblance to the economic process. The thermodynamic concepts of energy, force, and matter always had an immediate use-value: energy was force used to move matter. Thermodynamics must first be understood as a performative phenomenology of the steam engine, and from its beginnings in the early nineteenth century the discipline was overwhelmingly concerned with designing devices to induce heat in order to produce work. In Maxwell's briefest definition, thermodynamics is 'the theory of heat as a form of energy' (9). Maxwell's *Theory of Heat* is misnamed, for in thermodynamics thermal theory and economic practice are indistinguishable. Thermodynamics was an economy of steam, accounting for the production, distribution, and consumption of steam (the Maxwell demon goes so far as to perform all three functions at once) at the very moment that steam took up a central position in the economic process. In 1824 Sadi Carnot founded the discipline by working out a problem which, like the Maxwell demon, involved a bicameral compartment in a steam vessel. So radical is the equivalence between work and heat in thermodynamics that, in its First Law, the discipline does not even distinguish work performed from heat generated.[16]

Almost as soon as scientists formulated a working definition of the entropy law, they began to imagine situations that violated it. Carnot himself conceived of the first of many imaginary reversals of the entropic process. The Maxwell demon was by far the best-known of these reversals, as well as the most fantastic. The project that animated these models was the construction of a machine in which the entropic process could be contained and even reversed. But the two models differed markedly in the means they assembled to reverse entropy. In Carnot's engine, entropy, or the direction of heat transference, could only be reversed through the expenditure of a massive amount of mechanical work. For his part, Carnot openly admitted that the energy produced by the entropy reversal would probably not be worth the energy expended in producing it; that the resulting control over entropy would at best be partial.[17] In Maxwell's system, however, a magical sorting demon performed the reversal and the control over entropy was complete. The common element uniting these two models was that they differed little in their assessment of the resources necessary to produce an entropy reversal. In Carnot's system the control of entropy would appear to require so much energy that only a confederation of the scale of a polity could afford to undertake it. Maxwell's system also sanctioned the possibility of controlling entropy by making it appear that entropy could be controlled if only – through a crash program in research and development, a sort of Victorian Manhattan Project – the right technology could somehow be found and deployed. In both cases, the clear implication was that only a large-scale endeavor orchestrated by state institutions would have any chance at all of controlling the entropic process.

The state control of the entropic process, then, was the only form of control over entropy encompassing enough to be potentially counter-entropic. The control that nineteenth-century states achieved over entropy never amounted to much, but a variety of attempts contributed to the formation of a mythology of state control over knowledge in which the dream of controlled entropy played a central role. Jules Verne had a team of scientists journey to the center of the earth in order to harness a knowledge of the planet's heat as a source of power for European nations. A few years later Britain and France sent teams of scientists to study the thermal effects of the 1883 Krakatoa eruption, and in the 1890s both countries established weather bureaus.[18] In each of these instances the project of control failed, stymied by the number of variables at play and by the inability to arrive at a series of compatible control variables. The reach of state control had again exceeded its grasp. Thermodynamics well understood that measurement could no longer be considered the measure of control, that the increase of entropy in nature was irreversible. Unquestionably Maxwell intended his demon to illustrate that, though understood mechanistically, entropy could not form the basis for a machine. It did not take long for the search for an entropy machine (for inducing order) to shade logically into research on an entropy weapon (for inducing disorder). It would take forty years and require the stress of war before the German High Command introduced its secret entropy weapon, poison gas, into the theater of war. But it proved to be the most unreliable weapon in history. Gas simply did not conform to the solid and fluid mechanical systems that had long regulated warfare. The thermodynamics experts who developed mustard gas had found it hard to handle even under controlled conditions. Outdoors, subject to the thermal vicissitudes of the weather, the movement of the gas became completely nonlinear. Though regulated by a few simple general equations, the gas's velocity, pressure, density, and viscosity defied all prediction. The wind blew the gas in both directions and entropy became chaos.[19]

The drift of entropy had long been imagined as the primary constituent of a global chaos. In 1884 a perception of the nonlinearity of gaseous motion inspired Ruskin to give a lecture called 'The Storm-Cloud of the Nineteenth Century.' Ruskin sees in the weather evidence for entropy on a global scale. Everywhere he looks he sees an increase in storms, winds, and rain. Instead of the order of things attributed to nature within the Victorian museum (the lens through which, as shown in the first chapter, he was accustomed to view the world), Ruskin finds in the weather a thermodynamic phenomenon which brings forces into play that radically alter ordinary mechanistic representations of nature. Throughout the lecture he assembles an inventory of metaphors of heat and wind without ever realizing that what he faces, and most fears, is entropy. The progress toward entropy in Ruskin's lecture is exemplary, and the 'essential signs' of 'the phenomena characteristic of the plague-wind' move rapidly from natural theology to thermodynamics: first 'it is a wind of darkness'; second 'it is a malignant *quality* of wind, unconnected with any one quarter of the compass' that 'blows indifferently from all'; third 'it always blows *tremulously*'; fourth 'it is also *intermittent* with a rapidity quite unexampled in former weather'; fifth 'it degrades, while it intensifies, ordinary storm.'[20] The movement is first malignant and deliberate, then it breaks apart and becomes unmeasurable and loses all traces of origin. Then it begins to blow unpredictably, first tremulously, then intermittently. In the end the wind figures the degradation of all ordered structures.[21] Like Dickens surveying the London fog in *Bleak House* (1851), the disorganization Ruskin perceives in the weather is not a contrary force opposed to order but the very absence of comprehensible order. Try as he might, Ruskin cannot take a reading of the state of the system at a given moment. In a thermodynamic universe, the entropic process has eroded the certainty of positive knowledge. Time no longer has transparent origins and history no longer has anthropocentric ends. The end Ruskin foresees is trivial, the result of a universe governed indifferently by the laws of chance and statistics.

For Ruskin, as for many late Victorians, what the entropic end of the universe really meant was the end of the British Empire. Thirty years before Eliot's Prufrock, Ruskin closes his lecture by meditating on that sunless entropic end: 'the Empire of England, on which formerly the sun never set, has become one on which he never rises.'[22] Here the heat-death of the universe has become the heat-death of the Empire. In Britain, the problem of the relation of order to disorder had long been understood as an internal problem of culture and anarchy. In a series of striking metaphors, Ruskin now translated the problem into an external relation of culture and entropy. The substitution was crucial, for Ruskin was among the first to see the expansion of England as an essentially entropic process. Meteorology was a science of global systems, and using the weather as his metaphorical base, Ruskin saw all global systems as passing from order to disorder. The difference is that while Arnold saw disorder as a destructive force existing outside order and threatening to destroy it, Ruskin, like the founders of Victorian thermodynamics, saw disorder as existing *inside* order as a first principle of order itself. Never a close student of science, Ruskin did not articulate this directly; mostly he used thermodynamic constructions indirectly as menacing images. Nevertheless, if Arnold took anarchy to be a fluctuation in systems of order, Ruskin worked from the assumption that entropy was *order by fluctuation*, a form of order understood as process rather than state. Entropy was not the negation of order but was rather order's negative, an organizing principle of disorder that only made sense when observed from on high. Ruskin's lecture thus presupposes the global direction of entropy even though, unlike the later analysis of J.A. Hobson in *Imperialism* (1902), he does not yet regard entropy as a basic feature of the economic process.[23]

'The Storm-Cloud of the Nineteenth Century' stands at a point of juncture in late Victorian culture because it reverses early optimistic assessments of the relation between entropy and information. For

Ruskin the prospect of controlled entropy pales beside the reality of 'the almost ceaseless action of this calamitous wind.'[24] Unlike Maxwell, Ruskin does not posit the existence of a demon. He does not believe that being informed about the entropic process helps to control or even to curtail it. Instead he sees himself as a more or less helpless custodian of information plotting the slope of entropy. Society he sees as a thermodynamic system whose performance can no longer be predicted; what knowledge he possesses about the weather cannot be resolved into a sequence of compatible statements. First articulated by Ruskin but later the object of a wide consensus, this idea of information as entropy shattered the ideology of comprehensive knowledge that had animated the project of the imperial archive in the late nineteenth century. After the 1880s perfect control over knowledge would continue to be important – but as an article of faith rather than as a principle of science. In the epistemology of the twentieth century, control over one information system would no longer be predicated on the existence of a system of systems. The scale of knowledge would decrease even as the domains of information increased and multiplied. And it would become harder and harder to view society itself as a system about which exact knowledge was possible. By the turn of the century, H.G. Wells, Britain's last great system-builder, would be able to write a novel predicated on the most influential idea in Victorian thermodynamics: that information is knowledge whose central condition has become entropy.

II

Tono-Bungay (1909) is a novel of entropy transformation. Wells was the first novelist to attempt to render the phenomenology of the entropy flow, or the feel of the process by which the producers of energy lay waste the stock of the earth's resources. The novel comprises a sequence of situations in which concentrated energy available for use (low entropy usually in the form of raw materials) has been systematically transformed into dispersed energy unavailable for use (high entropy in the form of expended matter).[25] Following Ruskin's lead, Wells views the entropic process as so basic to life on earth that it must necessarily be seen everywhere in the infrastructure of culture. Everywhere he looks, Wells sees societies as systems operating on matter to produce waste, and he goes so far as to see the construction of all social systems as predicated on the form of matter they consume as energy. In *Tono-Bungay* agriculture, mining, and manufacture all create and nearly exhaust specific modes for producing energy. In a variety of ways the novel anticipates the influential thesis of Frederick Soddy's *Matter and Energy* (1912), namely, that 'the relations between energy and matter . . . control, in the last resort, the rise or fall of political systems, the freedom or bondage of nations, the movements of commerce and industry, the origin of wealth and poverty and the general physical welfare of the race.'[26] For Wells the construction of knowledge within the British Empire always depends on the type and amount of energy consumed. In *Tono-Bungay* the British Empire is less a political configuration than an imperium of matter assembled to produce energy. In the Victorian Britain of James Clerk Maxwell, the word 'power' had come to mean not only the control of authority but also the capacity for exerting force by consuming energy. For the Edwardian England in which Wells acted as a primary spokesman, the practice of power now became inseparable from the knowledge of energy.

The leading theorists of Victorian thermodynamics had all largely regarded their new science as a physics of economic value. Wells works within this central problematic of obtaining the highest output of work from a given form of energy, but he carries the economic implications of thermodynamics so much further that *Tono-Bungay* may well be regarded as a foundational fictional text of econometrics. In every way possible the novel places the trajectory of entropy at the center of the economic process. Essentially Wells views the productive base of human societies as a regulative structure of sentient Maxwell demons staving off entropy, not by reversing it (that cannot be done), but by reorganizing it in one way or another. *Tono-Bungay* traces the historical life cycles of the technologies of British agriculture, manufacture, and mining. The novel begins with an anatomy of an imperilled agricultural system, 'the Bladesover system.' It then turns to an extended parody of entropy in the manufacturing process, embodied in the patent medicine system of turn-of-the-century Britain. It ends with the collapse of a scheme for monopolizing a mineral resource. Paradoxically, as will become clear, Wells sees this exhaustion of resources as a sign of vitality in human affairs. The wreckage of outmoded technologies for exploiting nature may blight the planet, but it is precisely what paves the way for new constructions of science, science fictions which, given enough time, become science facts. In Wells's view the entropic exhaustion of various systems for exploiting the planet's energy resources is what engenders new systems for placing the remaining resources in what was later called a 'negentropic' configuration. He thus sets up his novel as a series of overlapping entropies within the capitalist economic process of Britain, each of which constantly eludes complete control even as it places immense pressure on the British social system to generate new procedures for partial and temporary control.

The Bladesover system of *Tono-Bungay* is a fossil embedded in the capitalist world economy in which Wells sees Britain as prime mover. The novel's narrator, George Ponderevo, repeatedly underscores the narrowly systemic character of agrarian England, the England of his childhood. 'The great house, the church, the village, and the labourers and the servants in their stations and degrees, seemed to me, I say, to be a closed and complete social system. About us were other villages and great estates, and from house to house, interlacing, the Gentry, the fine Olympians, came and went. The country towns seemed mere collections of shops . . . this was the order of the world.'[27] This is the public sphere as miniature, a form of representation which Susan Stewart has seen as 'linked to nostalgic versions of childhood and history' and presenting 'a diminutive, and thereby manipulable, version of experience, a version which is domesticated and protected from contamination.'[28] In *Tono-Bungay* Wells gives the miniature a specific thermodynamic cast. Wells's miniature model of Britain is a highly stratified but isolated structure of domination, a closed system in which the axial division of labor is so ordered that the system has begun to exhibit diminishing returns. Unlike George Gissing in *The Private Papers of Henry Ryecroft* (1903), W.H. Hudson in *Green Mansions* (1904), or Rudyard Kipling in *Puck of Pook's Hill* (1906), Wells makes no attempt to celebrate agrarian life. He sees agriculture as a form of entropy, exhausting the land and allowing a feudal society to survive in a marginal zone of the capitalist economy. Though the Bladesover system appears to present Wells with a permanent world, he saw that even an economy predicated on renewable resources cannot renew itself indefinitely. In small and then in large ways, entropy, with all of its attendant problems of probability and prediction, sets in.

The immediate and primary alternative to the agrarian Bladesover system in *Tono-Bungay* is the manufacture of commodities. For Wells the manufacturing sector offers yet another object lesson in the irrevocability of the entropic process. In the patent medicine system of Wells's Edwardian England, there is a continuous and irreversible degradation of free into bound energy. In the novel this degradation takes place under the direction of Edward Ponderevo, George's uncle. The elder Ponderevo devotes his energies to defeating the entropy law by bootlegging low entropy with the aid of some ingenious contrivances. The way Ponderevo gets something for nothing is by making and selling things that nobody needs. An individual buying Tono-Bungay (the name of Ponderevo's patent medicine) represents an act of pure expenditure. For society at large it represents a massive squandering of resources, for, as Wells recognizes, capitalism entails not merely the capacity to produce commodities but also the power to amass value in the form of capital. In *Tono-Bungay* the most excruciating forms of waste all result from the wasteful deployment of capital which Wells, along with other socialists like Rosa Luxemburg, sees as following its own internal logic of accumulation and diversification. The British economy moves inexorably from the solidity of things, from which it is still possible to derive a labor theory of value, to the amorphousness – the literal social formlessness – of capital, in which all value manifests a tautological dependence on further constructions of value. For the result of what Wells's captain of commerce calls 'a romantic exchange of commodities' (111) is the systemic waste resulting from the accumulation process in high capitalist England.

The massive centralization of resources in 'the modern man of power' (220) acts only as a temporary counter against the force of entropy. The great consortium of corporations, private investors, central banks, and international agencies that forms a protective circle of courtiers around the figure of the sovereign capitalist in *Tono-Bungay*, merely succeeds in organizing a social structure for temporarily resolving the contradictions of an entropic economy. These contradictions ran like a fault line across Edwardian Britain, and the social critics of the time did not require formal training in thermodynamics to see them. C.F.G. Masterman's *The Condition of England* (1909) had revived the mid-Victorian Condition-of-England debates by reformulating them in explicitly entropic terms. 'The whole of modern life has the accusation resting upon it, that it is moved by no ideal inner springs.'[29] There is no better image of the closed idealism that always informed and pervaded the mechanical world picture, a picture that tended to represent the economic process as a mechanical operation. The mechanistic epistemology had been responsible for a conception of the economic process, shared alike by bourgeois and radical political economists, as a closed system or circular flow. In striking contrast Masterman looks around him and sees a chaos of waste, not only of human resources (the usual subject of earlier Condition-of-England debates), but of natural resources (for which he offers 'the law of diminishing returns in agriculture' as a universal parallel). For Masterman the economic process is not circular but unidirectional; it leads 'to the scrap heap'(27). Like Wells, whose narrator deliberates whether he should change his novel's name from *Tono-Bungay* to *Waste*, Masterman sees the economic process as consisting of a continuous transformation of low entropy into high entropy, into irrevocable waste, into the various forms of what we now call pollution. It had begun to be widely recognized that an entire domain of material activity – waste production – had been completely left out the calculus of the productive process, a domain of activity that had actually acted as a prime determinant in forming and directing that process. To an extent that few political economists had foreseen, the system of capitalist production had become a stay against its entropic by-products.

This conclusion had forced itself on one of the most prescient of Victorian political economists, Stanley Jevons, whose *The Coal Question* (1866), a text in the tradition of Malthusian political economy, attempted to pose the question of the total carrying capacity of the planet. Jevons avoids using the concept of entropy in its popular sense as an annunciation of the end of the world, what Clausius had called the final 'heat-death' of the universe. For Jevons the impending scarcity of coal is not a manifestation of global entropy but the clear result of attempts to reduce it. He sees that the problem is that, although the earth's thermal energy can be consumed mechanically, it cannot be produced mechanically. Mechanical manipulation is not capable of acting in perpetual motion without a source of energy to produce motion. 'Coal has all those characteristics which entitle it to be considered the best natural source of motive power. It is like a spring, wound up during geological ages for us to let down.'[30] Yet far from being a no-strings-attached gift of pure negentropy, the release of this pent-up energy always results in an increase of entropy in the surrounding environment. If entropy is, by definition, energy unavailable for use, it also partly consists, Jevons recognizes, of expended energy that actively interferes with the use of other and newer forms of energy (to use an obvious example, the thermal effects of air pollution make it more difficult to harness the sun's radiation). In other words, Jevons sees the exhaustion of one form of energy as a bar to using other forms of energy. In *The Coal Question* there is no longer such a thing as free energy, an idea which begins to look like the old dream of perpetual motion in modern dress. The conclusion forced on Jevons is that the reserves of energy will soon be exhausted and that new reserves of energy must be found elsewhere in the world. He ends his book with a new kind of call to empire, a call that has since become a war cry: an ecological call for the seizure of new resources, a call based on the dwindling resources of the home economy.

The search for new domains of natural resources often came close to turning Victorian political economists into dowsers. So many substances – animal, vegetable, and mineral – with almost magical properties went in and out of fashion between the 1860s and the First World War that it is easy to see why, in *Tono-Bungay*, H.G. Wells makes an explicit leap from the manufacture of patent medicines to the discovery of magic resources. Patent medicine, heir to alchemy, and mining for raw materials, heir to gold prospecting, are both fantasies of free energy. Early in Wells's novel the medicine promises to deliver bodily energy in the form of vitality, while, near the end, a scheme for harnessing the energy contained in a substance called 'quap' promises to deliver mechanical energy in the form of 'a festering mass of earths and heavy-metals, polonium, radium, ythorium, thorium, cerium, and new things too' (183). Quap is the patent medicine of raw materials, the cure-all substance with the secret formula, a form of low entropy freed from dependence on agriculture, mining, or manufacture. The younger Ponderevo begins by trying to retrieve quap because of its 'rarity value' (186) and ends by realizing that its value is of a different and inestimable order. He represents quap as pure low entropy requiring very little human labor to process it; like later utopian projects for feeding the world on seaweed, he envisions a world whose energy needs have been met by a decaying substance that just happens to have washed ashore. In a very real sense quap is radium, petroleum, hydroelectric power, atomic energy, cold fusion, all rolled into one energetic symbol of the search for free energy in the twentieth-century imagination. In an 1886 essay, Ludwig Boltzmann said that free energy is the object of the struggle for life.[31] By placing the quest for quap at the center of his novel, Wells also sees that the modern philosopher's stone has become the magical transformation of energy from high to low states of entropy.

The final outcome of *Tono-Bungay* points to the flaws in this fantasy of entropy-free exchange in societies operating under a capitalist regime of value. The wastefulness of their enterprises eventually catches up with the two Ponderevos, despite the nephew's attempts to rationalize the patent medicine concern along Taylorist lines so as to counter his uncle's irrational business practices. The rationalized overconsumption of commodities in consumer societies like Edwardian Britain speeds up the rate at which the earth's resources approach exhaustion. By linking the collapse of the Ponderevo patent medicine empire with the failed scheme for cornering all the world's quap, Wells comes very close to regarding low entropy as the most basic form of capital. In the 1860s Marx certainly had regarded the capitalist economy as founded on the capital of low entropy with which the planet is endowed; the *Grundrisse* is essentially an anatomy of the process by which the earth's resources are transformed into commodities.[32] Although Marx does not go so far as to place absolute and inexorable ecological limits on capitalist expansion, he is perfectly aware that free energy cannot be used more than once. Just as a crop cannot be indefinitely reproduced on the same piece of land, so the Californias and South Africas of the world cannot go on yielding minerals forever. Marx did not live long enough to join in the late-Victorian project of grounding his economic laws governing exchange in objective laws of matter, to respond to a new feature introduced by Wells and others into the theory and practice of exchange under world capitalism: the entropic character of exchange.

The labor theory of value was a theory of value transmitted without loss. Marx saw exchange as increasing the value of commodities and made this increase into the basis of *Capital*'s most famous equation, M–C–M'. But Wells places entropy at the heart of the economic process. The labor theory of value was a theory of value derived from labor, and labor alone. Marx reduces value to the labor of human beings and not to the resources provided by the environment. Though Marx was perfectly aware of how, in practice, human beings exploited natural resources and, in so doing, exploited each other (as in his account of the California gold rush), he tended to take natural resources themselves as a given. But overall the capital provided by low entropy simply does not enter into the equation: not only does Marx follow the classical economists in leaving natural resources out of his account of the economic process, but he repeatedly stresses that everything nature offers us is free.[33] In the thermodynamic construction of the exchange process, however, the increase of value that takes place through the act of exchange always and necessarily relies on an increase in the entropy of the surrounding environment. Here value takes on value not only by taking it from human labor but also by draining it from the surrounding environment. Put simply, value creates waste, and waste impels the search for new constructions of value.

This search has always had global import and impact. The environment from which value partially derives its value conforms to no national border. Wells sees entropy as an imperial order of value that always creates new geographies of capital. As a historian in *The Outline of History* (1921), anticipating the work of the Annales School, Wells sees entropy migration as one of the great motive forces in history. He takes particular interest in the wars fought by nations for control of the world's natural resources. From the Mongol migrations across the Steppes in the thirteenth century to the exhaustion of the European forests in the fifteenth century, from the waves of immigration out of Europe in the nineteenth century to the impending exhaustion of the Amazon rain forest in the twentieth century, Wells would see natural resources not as a given but as a peculiarly human invention.[34] Others can and will be invented and used up, and in his science fiction Wells holds out the hope that, in the long run, the periodic table of the elements may not be closed but open-ended.[35] But in the short run he recognizes that there is always a struggle for actually existing resources. If, for Wells, low entropy is the most basic form of capital, the impending exhaustion of the British stock of low entropy through 'one vast dismal spectacle of witless waste' (284) must soon lead to a crisis in British world hegemony. In *Tono-Bungay* young Ponderevo has to resort to violence, killing a black inhabitant of East Africa to obtain the low entropy – the quap – he so desperately needs to restore his uncle's business empire to economic viability. At the outer reaches of the entropically expanding imperium resides the necessity of force.

Tono-Bungay, then, is a parable of Britain coming to terms with the entropic character of the world capitalist economic process. The capitalism he represents has no settled order or trajectory; it cannot be fully explained by the best efforts of classical Marxism; it borders on a chaos of waste, 'a confusion of casual accidents' (82). In *Tono-Bungay*, all production represents a deficit in entropy terms. The capitalist system can no longer be approached as Newton approached the behavior of the heavenly bodies, seeking their immutable laws of motion. In Wells's novel, rather, capitalism takes on a new kind of order. It appears not as an economic system but as an economic process capable of reconfiguring the very terms under which it operates. In *Capital* Marx saw this when he argued that the commodity form must itself be considered not as a *forma formata* but as a *forma formans*.[36] The boom-and-bust cycles of capitalism had often led others also to call attention to its aperiodicity and unpredictability. What sets Wells apart from these theorists is that he regards the capitalist economic process as a system that never sorts itself out and enters a steady state. Rather it makes and breaks many connections between many kinds of systems, semiotic systems (such as advertising), organizations of power (such as the state), means of production (such as raw materials), and modes of production (such as the factory system). This process can assume many different forms, but it continually shatters any sense of fixity that would make it possible to know the system, as a system, in its totality. In *Tono-Bungay* the economic process has become as familiar, and yet as hard to predict and control, as the weather.

The problem of achieving a unitary capitalism in *Tono-Bungay* takes the form of the fracturing of information through advertising. From its inception as a major institution of capitalism in the late nineteenth century, advertising functioned not only as a means of publicity but also as a fantasy of information control. The institution had achieved prominence as a massive attempt to control the entropic character of the capitalist economic process by setting up conduits for manipulating the transmission of knowledge in the public sphere. The most crucial, and the least appreciated, of advertising's ideological functions in the late nineteenth century was quite simply its ability to persuade people that it actually worked. In the chaos of capitalism, advertising proposed an achieved discursive order. It restored the appearance of purposive activity to the volleying dialectic of entropic and counter-entropic forces in the capitalist world system. In advertising all accumulation always appears to entail further accumulation; loss does not enter into the equation at all. The overall picture of exchange constructed by advertising must be seen as yet another version of those visions of free exchange against which Wells, in incident after cumulative incident in his novel, mobilizes the forces of entropy.

Wells sets the whole of his novel in marked opposition to the interested self-representations of the advertising industry. In *Tono-Bungay* the transmission of information has been severed from the possibility of reciprocal communication. The elder Ponderevo consistently latches onto forms of communication that have large capacities for transmitting information – clichés, buzz words, catch phrases. For Ponderevo the problem of transmitting a message via advertising is, for all practical purposes, independent of whether the message has any vital importance or is wholly nonsensical (the ads reproduced in the novel often border on nonsense). Actual consumers do not enter into any of his calculations. In essence Ponderevo has constructed a one-way system of communication that lacks the basic component of any control system, namely, a feedback process. As advertising, language approaches the condition of pure noise, for Ponderevo conceives of advertising as an undirected message spreading out until it finds a receiver. In other words, he conceives of communication as a purely statistical act in which sales somehow result from an overwhelming number of collisions among consumers interacting with large bodies of information. He is not a kind of capitalist Maxwell demon sorting information to place the capitalist market into some pattern of regularity. In Wells's novel advertisements have become not a counter to entropy but an index of entropy, not just in the natural world but in the public sphere at large.

The novel thus provides us with a remarkably prescient explanation of how, in Edwardian England, the concept of entropy negotiated its passage from the theory of energy consumption to the theory of information. For in *Tono-Bungay* the primary example of the entropic degradation of ordered structures accompanying the exhaustion of various sources of energy (agricultural in the Bladesover system, mineral in the quap episode, manufacturing in the patent medicine factory) turns on the entropy of information through advertising. This linkage of energy and information points to a moment when the idea of entropy had begun to take on a new dimension. The puzzle of Maxwell's demon gave the illusion that a machine for processing information about various sorts of molecules could, first, be run at very little cost, and, second, counter entropy. Properly positioned, a sentient being or machine could indefinitely reverse the direction of entropy. The problem here becomes one of agency: who or what power is capable of bringing about such a reversal? Wells devotes much of his novel to showing how an information machine run by an independent capitalist entrepreneur like old Ponderevo fails to counter entropy (advertising instead appears as a form of knowledge whose central condition has become entropy), and in the end advances it considerably. The only viable alternative he presents to capitalist chaos entails a different kind of information machine run by a different kind of functionary: the state scientist.

The counter-entropic forces of the novel subsist in the figure of the younger Ponderevo, the state scientist in whose hands Wells places the project of a mechanistic epistemology confronting the hard fact of entropy in a thermodynamic world. Despite his considerable scientific sophistication, George Ponderevo inhabits, and seeks to render secure against intrusion, a Newtonian universe of projectiles. George clearly views his universe of scientific knowledge as radically different from the world of patent medicines: his work is 'of an altogether different sort from that of Tono-Bungay' (11). Though he consistently sets his own work apart from his uncle's, and though their world-views are in part very different, the two projects are in fact informed by complementary mechanistic ideologies set apart by the subsidy structure of the modern state, which intervenes to recast classical mechanics at the very moment when, due to the introduction of thermodynamics, it no longer appears tenable as a vehicle for control.

The breakdown of old Ponderevo's mechanistic epistemology runs an interference pattern across *Tono-Bungay*. Wells consistently aligns old Ponderevo with an obsolete mechanical world-view. At one point he designs 'The Ponderevo Patent Flat, a Machine you can Live in' (47). In another remarkable passage old Ponderevo says that Kipling's 'Below the Mill Dam' is his favorite work of fiction. This is a story about an inefficient old dam that must be rebuilt to produce hydroelectric power; it explores a situation common in engineering, namely, the attempted use of mechanization to counter the limitations of classical mechanics. Victorian engineering had repeatedly come up against practical limits to Newtonian mechanics.[37] In 1870s America railway bridges were collapsing at the rate of twenty-five a year; other structures were thought to be near collapse (think of the fear the creaking of the hull provokes in Conrad's *Lord Jim* [1900]). Following the collapse of the Tay Bridge in 1879 due to changes in barometric pressure, engineers had begun to question Newton's third law of motion, which states that if the status quo is maintained then all the forces on an object must cancel each other out. In the terms of Newton's third law the bridge, like the sealed bulkheads in the *Titanic*, had been mathematically perfect, a truly rigid solid designed to balance a variety of internal forces. The problem is that this law does not say anything about how these various forces are generated, or about the degree to which forces, once generated, interact with inanimate solids. In Newtonian mechanics the distinction between force and matter is as pronounced as the separation of subject and object in Lockean epistemology. The continual adjustments of tension in seemingly solid matter brought about by dynamic interaction with the object's immediate thermal environment – the basis for theorizing thermodynamics – does not enter into the picture at all.

It was precisely a synthesis of postulates from solid tensor mechanics and gaseous pressure dynamics that paved the way for mechanized flight (fundamentally an airplane is a thermodynamic projectile). In *Tono-Bungay* George Ponderevo reacts to his uncle's valorization of basic classical mechanics by trying to update mechanics by designing flying machines. He works out 'a series of problems connected with the stability of bodies pitching in the air and the internal movements of the wind' (225). This thoroughgoing conflation of the terms of classical mechanics and thermodynamics is central to the turn-of-the-century project of entropy reversal, for young Ponderevo believes that the forces of entropy can be countered by constructing machines that take thermodynamic forces into account. For Ponderevo a machine is a Maxwell demon that orders disorder. He sees himself as part of a general mobilization of science to govern nature in order to govern the world. But as happens in Kipling, knowledge that begins as a great game ends as a form of strategy. He begins the novel by carrying on scientific research as a hobby and ends it by designing destroyers, all the while claiming that 'X2 isn't for the empire, or indeed for the hands of any European power' (317). Essentially he wants to occupy the entire sphere of knowledge in a movement that resembles a conquest or military invasion – not of any one country but of all space and time.

A mechanistic ideology of perfect control thus consistently animates young Ponderevo's synthesis of mechanics and thermodynamics. In *Tono-Bungay* this attempted synthesis takes place under the canopy of the state. Young Ponderevo repeatedly complains that the control exercised by the state over social systems does not extend nearly far enough; he wants to do away with 'the dingy underworld of the contemporary state' (255) and agrees with the proposition that all science 'ought to be under the State' (283). Wells sees scientists, even partially independent scientists like Ponderevo, as operating in the vanguard of state science. Like most state scientists, Ponderevo is concerned more with the production of knowledge than with its transmission (usually to the military), and he describes his production of knowledge in what can only be described as epic terms (as Lyotard has observed, states always spend large amounts of money to enable science to pass itself off as an epic). The project of *Tono-Bungay* represents Britain pivoting toward achieving a complete measure of control not only over its domain of socio-scientific knowledge but also over the economic process in its totality. Here the reassertion of the mechanical world-view becomes a means for countering entropy by controlling the economic process. As the novel ends, the clear implication is that in 'the State of To-morrow' advertising will no longer exist. As Wells's fellow socialist Sidney Webb pointed out in 1914, 'it will not be swayed by any consideration of individual gain; it will be directed by persons acting only as the servants of the particular branches of public adminis-tration concerned.'[38] This is yet another vision of a fully controlled state apparatus organized around a series of exact and encompass-ing definitions of what constitutes knowledge, a system of systems in which socialist advertising plays the role of a Maxwell demon able to separate various kinds of information for the public good. It continues to work within the framework of an imagined total knowledge of a system, a knowledge that always turns out to be not complete and descriptive but fragmented and prospective, not achieved but planned.

For most of his life Wells attempted to distance himself from Ponderevo's ideology of comprehensive social control. It comes under scrutiny in Wells's *Outline of History* (1921), much of which deals with the weakness of state and socioeconomic bureaucracies. Here Wells's discussion of the simultaneously open and closed information economy of Renaissance Venice is exemplary. There, Wells relates, an extraordinarily open network of communication, intranational and international (forming one of the chief sources of European history) accompanied an obsessive closure of the channels of state information, exaggerated to such an extent that the state ordered the assassination of itinerant artisans and other migrants to maintain its monopoly over the conduits of information. In this example a state apparatus intervenes with too heavy a touch, attempting to control an information subsystem by destroying it. This is an attempt to define knowledge as the state's concentrated monopoly capital in a world in which, as even old Ponderevo sees clearly enough in *Tono-Bungay*, the forces of the economy have become 'delocalized.' When he stops to look closely at the project of comprehensive knowledge, Wells is quite capable of seeing all attempts to assemble knowledge encyclopedically as little more than paralogies of control.[39]

Yet undeniably Wells is in fact the last inheritor of the dogmatism of a unified and systematic knowledge whose conditions and possibility he renounces. Though in fiction and science fiction Wells parodies the efforts of those who attempt to round off the partial systems of the world into a totality, his own practice as a historian reveals a search for a complete knowledge of the world. Though Wells distances himself from the idea that the world can be brought under control, he sees in world history something that can be outlined. He wrote *The Outline of History* 'primarily to show that *history as one whole* is amenable to a more broad and comprehensive handling than is the history of special periods and nations,' a treatment in which 'as the outlook broadens, the clustering multitude of details dissolves into general laws.'[40] In other words, he replaces a model of exact positive knowledge with a model of inexact synoptic knowledge. As he grew older Wells became more and more inclined to assert the program of comprehensive knowledge as a guarantor of stability. In 1938 he proposed beginning a 'World Encyclopedia' as an explicitly counter-entropic project, 'to bring human ecology into one correlated survey,' 'a comprehensive conception of the world.'[41] Wells does not set the world up as a picture, an object-world like that of the nineteenth-century Great Exhibitions, but as a series of rapid successive frames of knowledge grouped into an encyclopedia.[42] He proposes maintaining knowledge not as a totality frozen in time and space, but as a quasi-totality developing through time and moving in space. The reason he selects the encyclopedia as the ideal form for the kind of comprehensive knowledge he has in mind is because it preserves the conception of a complete knowledge even as, decade after decade, it expands into new editions, growing larger and less complete while still preserving something of Hegel's idea that an encyclopedia ought to form a circle of circles. In Wells the comprehensive world-view refuses to compose itself into a picture but settles quite easily onto one broad line.

The remarkable argument of *The Outline of History* is that the slope of the line of historical development runs downward into entropy, levelling out in what Wells terms the most massive dispersal of resources in history, 'the catastrophe of 1914,' only to take a sudden upward turn to culminate in 'Our true State, this state that is already beginning, this state to which every man owes his utmost political effort, [which] must be now this nascent Federal World State to which human necessities point.'[43] Wells does not say how such a perfect state will come about, but he makes it clear that he sees this future system as a steady state of affairs in which order begets order. This is a nostalgia for the very Bladesover system he calls obsolete. A forerunner of many people in the mid twentieth century who wished that they could turn back the clock and disinvent nuclear energy, Wells yearns for the re-establishment of enduring ordered structures. In *Tono-Bungay* there is an uncanny symmetry between the entropy-steadiness of the Bladesover system at the beginning of the novel, and that of the universal state apparatus at the end. What Wells's Ponderevo really wants is a new and better Bladesover system ruled by science, capable of rejuvenating itself indefinitely, not simply violating the Second Law of Thermodynamics but actively refuting it, showing once and for all that human beings can refuse to be governed by the laws of entropy transformation.

The ambivalence Wells felt toward the laws of thermodynamics calls to mind the impact of the many extensions of evolutionary theory on Victorian thought. As a myth of knowledge, entropy, like evolution, would seem to place history outside the domain of human activity. Because it transfers agency from human beings to physical principles, it ostensibly represents a pessimistic relinquishing of all the possibilities of social control. In *The Decline of the West* (1929) Oswald Spengler certainly thought that 'the myth of entropy signifies . . . the world's end as completion of an inwardly necessary evolution.'[44] Though the imagery of entropy certainly filtered into the bleak rhetoric of social prophecy as in the above case of Ruskin, it in fact served a far more complex function. It did not abolish human agency but rather transferred it to those elites who possessed the technology to manipulate physical laws, elites represented as superhuman. In late Victorian Britain social control was sometimes imagined as vitalism. 'Vitalism' was a representation of the self as a limitless reservoir of energy, of negentropy; at base it represented an organism successfully able to consume greater energy than it could produce.[45] The project of vitalism ran completely counter to the First Law of Thermodynamics, for it postulated that under no circumstances can energy ever be conserved, that it must always be spent, squandered, wasted. Vitalism was an attempt to reassert human control over the vastly expanding and rapidly entropying domains of information by defining all excess as inherent in human rather than natural activity, and the product of deliberation rather than confusion. By constructing a model of a body replete with excess of life force, a body that can out-machine machines, vitalism stands not only as one of the unacknowledged progenitors of cybernetics, but also as a refusal to be governed by the laws of entropy at the very moment when that governance first began to be perceived as absolute.

III

The Maxwell demon was an early prototype for what came to be called 'governor' technologies. A sequence of relays designed to direct a ship's rudder, the governor was, as Norbert Wiener has recognized, the beginning of cybernetics, the first unified system of feedback technology using the rapid transmission of information to counter entropy (the Victorian masters of thermodynamics both owe their greatest fame to their work on information systems, Kelvin on the transatlantic cable and Maxwell on the demon conundrum). In a very real sense, as the name implies, the 'governor' was also a prototype for a servo-engineered government of economy and society. In *Tono-Bungay* Wells pays homage to Maxwell when he ends his novel with young Ponderevo designing guidance mechanisms for destroyers and imagining the day when Britain will become an interlocking system of control mechanisms, a governor apparatus, what today has routinely come to be called a 'state apparatus.' Ponderevo, and perhaps Wells himself, did not foresee the day when the machine would lose its pre-eminence as a paradigm of knowledge and control, a day when, not too far in the future, knowledge would produce not only the known but the unknown, not only the controlled but the uncontrollable. 'If,' wrote James Clerk Maxwell in 1868, 'by altering the adjustments of the machine, its governing power is continually increased, there is generally a limit at which the disturbance, instead of subsiding more rapidly, becomes an oscillating and jerking motion, increasing in violence till it reaches the limit of the action of the governor.'[46]

Gravity's Rainbow rides a fine line along the conception of the apparatus and its paradoxical threshold of control: there comes a point at which control apparatuses lower the performance they claim to raise. Today the term 'feedback' has shifted its meaning from a completed to an interrupted act of communication (usually it means an information system catastrophically overloaded with energy). Pynchon sees the world precisely as a set of feedback apparatuses that have become completely incompatible. Among them, thermodynamics continues to play a major role, and in a variety of ways Pynchon, like Wells before him, pushes the project of Victorian thermodynamics about as far as it can go as a dominant paradigm of knowledge and power. It appears as a principle of the capitalist economic process, the imperial administration apparatus, and the information nexus itself. But, as Maxwell perceived, there comes a point of diminishing returns beyond which even thermodynamics cannot project or protect the possibility of complete control. The imperial archive had defined the outer perimeters of its control over an imperium of matter by imagining that it could control entropy. In Pynchon's 'Zone' of 1944–45, the control of entropic processes encompasses only a limited portion of the observable world, and it does not even affect the control of a domain left out of Victorian thermodynamics, the unobservable world. In such a world 'entropy' is only one possible measure, and a fairly linear one at that, of the dynamic organization of energy, matter, and force. The new, nonlinear dimensions of control explored by Pynchon in *Gravity's Rainbow* announce what can only be considered a post-thermodynamic world.

The linear apparatus of thermodynamic feedback control is most clearly crystalized in the guidance apparatus of the rocket, the novel's central motif. The rocket's guidance system would seem best to conform to 'the Determination of the Number.'[47] The number functions to bring the performance of the rocket into an integrated whole. Numerical calculations tend to make nonlinear phenomena (especially thermodynamic phenomena) linear, or at least represent them using linear means. Calculations stipulate the frictive or delaying force that hampers the motion of the projectile. They plot the oscillations disturbing feedback to insure that it does not break down. They take into account the curvilinear prediction of flight (the rainbow arc of gravitational pull that is the novel's title). They determine not only economy of energy but also accurate reproduction of signal. They see to it that 'all is in order' (757). They perform the work of modernizing classical mechanics by taking into account random, statistical variation. Such calculations reduce all epistemology from theoretical to practical knowledge founded on instrumental reason. In all, they would seem to construct effectively working simulacra of motion, a world in which moving objects trace trajectories that can be broken into small segments and analyzed according to the method of Newton's calculus, a world of motive forces described with utter certainty by Newton in his *Principia* (1686) as 'absolute motion,' or 'the translation of a body from one absolute place into another' within a stable gravitating system.[48]

Despite the overwhelming presence of guidance and feedback systems in *Gravity's Rainbow*, nowhere in the novel does the ordering of pilot protocols assume such a neat deterministic structure. Pynchon consistently drives determination into the realm of overdetermination. Nowhere do machines function on their own, independent of human agency. Everywhere he looks Pynchon sees the widespread use of such devices as gyrocompass ship-steering systems (guiding the Argentinian submarine), anti-aircraft fire-control systems (protecting the city of Lübeck), automatically controlled oil-cranking stills (run by Shell Oil), thermostatic temperature equalizers (placed by electronics cartels), ultra-rapid computing machines (used by the White Visitation), and most prominently, self-propelled missiles. These automata contain in effect sense organs, effectors, and the equivalent of a nervous system – and they lend themselves very well to description in physiological terms (but they cannot replace them). Throughout the diaspora of the Zone, the Herero people of southwest Africa come to regard the circular insignia of 'the five positions of the launching switch in the A4 control car' as 'something deep, maybe a little mystical' (361). The novel ends in a scene of startling symbolic density in which Blicero launches the last V-2 of the Second World War. Sensing the insufficiency of the servomechanism as a device for the reception of impressions as well as the performance of actions, he turns the launch of Rocket 00000 into a ritual immolation of the boy Gottfried, bound in the capsule like a young girl in a Balinese fire ceremony. Blicero carefully omits the central feature of the governor apparatus, namely, two-way communication (he can speak to Gottfried but Gottfried cannot talk back to him). In this scene the machine's nervous system requires the presence of a human being to become fully proprioceptive. As in the old circus act of the human cannonball, ballistics remains curiously anthropocentric. The motion of bodies, far from being the ultimate in a Newtonian calculus of moving dead matter, has here become contingent on the movement of a single human body through time and space.

This conflation of control systems in *Gravity's Rainbow* completely undercuts the classical program of elaborating detailed and exhaustive mechanical models of phenomena. In Pynchon's novel a model is nothing more or less than a model, one framing device among many, a viewing platform, a point in time and space with no particular claim to privileged status. In the 1870s the Maxwell demon had constructed a model of knowledge as pure instrumentality in which the mechanisms of transmission, perception, and evaluation formed a unified field. Maxwell believed in the existence of isolated and highly stable systems whose performance could be predicted and controlled if only all the variables were known. Following the monism of the mechanistic epistemology, he believed that observation did not affect the observed phenomena, and that with the increased accuracy of instruments like the demon, it would finally prove possible to see things in their totality as they intrinsically are. At the turn of the century H.G. Wells replaced the Maxwellian model of pure instrumentality with a model of knowledge as mediated instrumentality in which the various mechanisms of information form a fragmented but nevertheless highly stable system (such as the Bladesover system) whose performance cannot be predicted even if all the variables are known. Here as elsewhere Wells incorporates a basic object lesson of modern physics, that every act of observation disturbs what it purports to observe, all the while retaining, in his encyclopedism, a sense that whatever this knowledge turns out to be, it ought to be made internally consistent by dint of a vitalistic will to comprehensive knowledge.

In the London of the 1940s Pynchon sees the end of control itself. In *Gravity's Rainbow* knowledges form not global unities but discrete and incommensurate subcultures. Pynchon incorporates the hard core of Heisenberg's Uncertainty Principle, namely, that it has become impossible for the observer to determine in which way, or by how much, observation disturbs the phenomena observed. He does not merely elevate objective laws of matter to metaphysical prominence as someone like Ruskin had done. Instead Pynchon realizes that the Heisenberg Uncertainty Principle expresses the inherent limitation of the human sensorium and its instrumental extensions. For Pynchon a mechanism of transmission is a mechanism of transmission, one of perception is one of perception, one of evaluation is one of evaluation. 'Information is information,' wrote Norbert Wiener in 1948, 'not matter or energy.'[49] Pynchon says it more vividly: 'The knife cuts through the apple like a knife cutting an apple' (758). The world is irreducibly fractional and cannot be molded into a noncontradictory framework. This is the heart of Niels Bohr's Principle of Complementarity, which states that phenomena can function with great consistency within entirely contradictory epistemologies. Just as the electron behaves both as a wave and as a particle – concepts irreducible to one another – so must a reader of Gravity's Rainbow be reconciled to the existence of mechanical, thermodynamic, and quantum phenomena side by side, and in complete opposition. But Pynchon complicates matters even further. Differing and opposed orders of information do not adhere to stable groupings in his novel. Centering around the figure of Slothrop, different orders of information continually interact to create new orders of information. Mathematics becomes chemistry becomes ballistics becomes cinema.[50] Formerly distinct knowledges once grouped into discrete specializations are transformed into relatively indistinct bodies of information that move like the turbulent flow of fluids. Nostalgic for a central ordering principle, Slothrop constantly suspects the presence of 'a reflex of order beyond the visible,' but before he can come up with a suitable totalizing explanation the ordering of orders fluctuates and sends the narrative off in a new direction. What troubles him most is that order seems to have become disorderly, uncontrollable, that direction no longer entails directedness, that the ordering of orders now exists without reference to an order of orders.

The control of knowledge in Gravity's Rainbow, then, has very largely become a non-control of information. Information is not unframed knowledge but knowledge framed provisionally in unstable data structures. James Clerk Maxwell had seen information as a way of establishing order against what he saw as the inevitable entropic degradation of ordered structures. H.G. Wells equated information with entropy rather than opposing them, and

in doing so accurately anticipated, as he so often did, later developments in science, notably Claude Shannon's 1949 theory of communication.[51] Thomas Pynchon speeds up the rate at which
information becomes entropic to such an extent that, in effect, he
displays the power of entropic obsolescence to mutate new technologies of control at a rapid rate. In *Gravity's Rainbow* the means of
partial control fall apart only to be replaced by new stopgap
measures of further partial control. What is controlled is of course
information, and in his novel this control is completely imaginary.
Indeed the control of information is so much of a fantasy that only
someone afflicted with paranoia could possibly believe in it. Pynchon sees paranoia as perhaps the final response to information out
of control. In *Gravity's Rainbow* paranoia is not a delusion, not a
measure of the distorting capacity of an individual human mind.
Paranoia is rather the belief that all information, far from continually breaking apart into disjoint fragments of fact, has an invisible
center and a true meaning. Paranoia is the modern sequel to
Victorian fantasies of a world united by information. Paranoia
reverses the degradation of knowledge into information. In paranoia all information becomes knowledge again, knowledge which
coheres as conspiracy. In the mind of the paranoid beholder, the
project of positive knowledge, forever pushing facts into disunion
and breaking them apart into particles of information, rejoins the
project of comprehensive knowledge, this time not as fantasy, as in
the imperial archive, but as delusion. The lineage of this delusion is
the subject of the next chapter.

FOUR

THE ARCHIVE AND ITS DOUBLE

This chapter looks at the double of the imperial archive: a library of comprehensive knowledge imagined outside the boundaries of state and empire, knowledge presumed to be the property of an enemy. From the 1870s until the First World War this enemy often changed shape, arrangement, location and nationality, and the nature of the knowledge attributed to enemies varied from useful to useless, from comprehensive to specialized, from everything to nothing. What remained constant was the apprehension that information systems designed by the state can be put to other, unintended uses. Whether undertaken by the museum, the university, or the geographical bureau, the project of amassing knowledge had usually presupposed not only an invisible interconnectedness among forms of knowledge but also a cultural cohesiveness among communities of knowers. Comprehensive knowledge was taken to be a nationalist project, initiated within national institutions (such as the British Museum or its counterpart in Kipling, the Lahore Museum), pursued by state functionaries (such as Kipling's Colonel Creighton), and like state sovereignty itself, presumed to be evenly operative over a legally demarcated territory (such as British India). In the nineteenth century, however, the production of information had taken on a new mobility. The control of dictionaries, encyclopedias and newspapers had passed from private bodies to large conglomerates. With top government administrators writing the latest articles for the *Encyclopaedia Britannica* (in Kipling's *Kim* [1901] one of the spies prepares to publish his report in the Proceedings of the Royal Society), all state secrets were increasingly open secrets. It was getting harder and harder to restrict knowledge to a given theater of operations. Knowledge itself had become a weapon in the Empire's arsenal, but a weapon of a new and flexible kind. What would happen if that knowledge fell into the wrong hands?

Since the end of the Napoleonic Wars the concert of Europe had depended on an epistemological levelling process. Keeping the peace meant maintaining a balance of power that was also a balance of knowledge. As yet the idea of a 'secret weapon' was inconceivable, for despite governmental pretensions of secrecy, reports of ballistics research circulated widely among the international scientific community.[1] The nineteenth-century idea of spying was not theft but infiltration; the aim was to know not what a state had done, but what it intended to do next (there were no monkey trials of Rosenbergs, accused of stealing plans for the atomic bomb, but of Dreyfuses, accused of penetrating the French high command). For the most part, maintaining an equilibrium of knowledge between the powers did not require the specialized services of spies.[2] The British government knew very well that those hostile to the Empire would merely have to read the latest proceedings of the Royal Geographical Society to see where the Foreign Office was concentrating its attention. To administer its Empire Britain had developed an open economy of local knowledge within which its operatives, working both in and out of the British Museum, produced and published so much information – linguistic studies, orientalist tracts, ethnographies, geographical reports – that only a large corporate or governmental entity could possibly possess the resources necessary to comprehend Britain's comprehensive knowledge. To a certain extent this surveillance was expected and even encouraged, for it contributed to the political equilibrium of nineteenth-century Europe; to a greater extent it was feared. Since the knowledge Britain was producing did not include what today we call 'disinformation' (the concept of deliberately circulated misinformation dates from the 1930s), the result was a massive problem of information control.[3]

The problem of controlling knowledge had always accompanied the project of amassing comprehensive knowledge, but around 1870 the problem of information control began to arouse more general concern than the specialized classification debates hitherto conducted by Darwin, Agassiz, Maxwell, and others. In January of 1871 the Hohenzollerns occupied the Versailles palace of the Bourbons and proclaimed a Prussian king the first Kaiser of the new

German Reich. Like the massive funding of the American university system following the Sputnik launch in 1957, the British reaction to the conclusion of the Franco–Prussian War was immediate and sustained. Almost immediately Lord Russell recommended the establishment of a new model army, and within a few years a Naval League had been formed to press for rearmament. The newly formed Education Boards now discovered a shortage of engineers and began to study the organization of Prussian scientific institutes. Everyone agreed that the Prussians, masters of both the knowledge of organization and the organization of knowledge, had evolved a parallel but alien construction of comprehensive knowledge that had to be interrogated at all costs. This construction was what can be called an enemy archive and it involved representing an enemy high command as pursuing some combination of dependent and independent research. In the nineteenth and twentieth centuries, the idea of the enemy archive served as an impetus to consolidate control over information by developing both new technologies of knowledge and new variants on the will to state power. It played a crucial role in the arms race that led up to World War I and contributed to a paranoia around information that has endured until this day.

The enemy archive was also a fantasy that produced a specialized literary genre and a new kind of individual, the corporate subject. In the summer of 1871 an anonymous story about a successful German invasion of England started a new genre that rarely rose above the generic. This new genre was the invasion novel.[4] Lieutenant-Colonel George Chesney's bestselling *The Battle of Dorking* performed a simple operation: it linked the control of territory with a hermeneutics of information. In this fiction, the first of hundreds of its kind, the area the state controls is exactly the same as the area it knows something about. Chesney comes right out and says that England lost the war because it was a poor curator of its own geographical knowledge. England could have prevailed, he says, had it been more familiar with its own territory. He is looking not for a great leader of warriors (a Napoleon) but for a great organizer of the knowledge and economy of war (an Eisenhower who, by his own admission, was a specialist in 'the procedure [by] which a nation's potential is transferred to its armed forces').[5] The novel is not a comic portrait of knowledge twisted in circles of statement and counter-statement – the world of Dickens's Circumlocution Office –

but a vision of knowledge that leads directly to power. More than anything else, *The Battle of Dorking* functioned as a call to arms arousing in its readers a sense of epistemological panic. Later invasion novels had titles like *The Channel Tunnel; or England's Ruin* and Trojan-horse plots of entry and occupation through conduits like tunnels, embankments, bridges, and ferries. They transformed the concert of Europe into a balance of terror and, early in 1871, succeeded in introducing a new verb into the English lexicon: to rearm.

But what emerges in the invasion novel is not just a call to arms but what can be called a war interiority: a field of human perception defined by the merging of the will to knowledge and the knowledge of war. In invasion novels the human mind works as hard as it can to gather information, reading the world around it for signs of a real or presumed enemy. The 'enemy' in question may not even be named or outlined in substance or shape. Rather, the hero of the invasion novel reads the visible world for evidence of an invisible but comprehensive design fraught with hostile intentions. His sensorium becomes a diorama of enemy contingency plans unfolding in time and space, and in turn he mobilizes each of his senses to discern contingency in the outside world. Design governs in small things, and the materially present world of sea, sand, sky, and air must be interpreted figurally for signs of conspiracy. Habitually the hero finds the large in the small, the readable in the illegible, the obvious in the recondite. This dual apprehension bound up within the war interiority – both a category of perception and a climate of fear – can be called epistemological paranoia. This kind of paranoia is neither a clinical phenomenon (Freud restricted paranoia to homosexual fears of exposure) nor an imaginary projection (today the word is largely used to connote unfounded suspicions about a hostile environment), but a thoroughgoing conflation of knowledge and terror. If, as Leo Bersani has written, 'paranoia is a necessary product of all information systems,' the product of a truly comprehensive information system, especially one presumed to be in enemy hands, would be a truly mind-boggling form of complete paranoia.[6] This is exactly what can be found in the invasion novel where, for the first time in literary history, the phenomenal world has been placed in a permanent state of red alert: in these fictions we can detect the first stirrings of the much-rehearsed nightmare scenario in which an ordinary event, a flock of birds flying south for the winter, could potentially be interpreted as a terrible threat by a radar network and so trigger nuclear armageddon.

This chapter argues that the invasion novel organized a corporate subject in whom was internalized an epistemological paranoia that can be seen as part of a larger and systematic phenomenology of rearmament. For at least a hundred years Britain had exercised an informal hegemony over the seas; now, in a remarkable series of representations, it sought to formalize that hegemony by making it a function of explicit military domination. The chapter first examines the problem of creating and controlling information systems for comprehensive knowledge, a problem foregrounded in Jules Verne's international bestseller *20,000 Leagues Under the Sea* (1870), a novel of epistemological terrorism written during the Franco–Prussian War and first translated into English in 1871 at the height of the rearmament scare. It then turns to the one masterpiece of the invasion genre, Erskine Childers's *The Riddle of the Sands* (1903), a novel imbued with the doctrine and delirium of military production and perception. It concludes with an analysis of military phenomenology in *Gravity's Rainbow* (1973), focusing on an episode in which Pynchon shows how certain archival techniques and practices of the 1930s and 1940s updated the invasion novel, as well as fashioning the ultimate paranoid corporate subject. Each of these fictions takes as its centerpiece the archival capabilities of a potential or presumed enemy and, in a decisive ideological move, depicts rearmament as an archival process. Each forms a real part of the history of the present, for the same realities that led to the invasion novel led to the Schlieffen Plan, led to D-Day, led to the most up-to-date forms of command mimesis, our automated defense systems, our strategies of deterrence, our war games, our ongoing state of emergency.

I

20,000 Leagues Under the Sea sets up an equation between epistemology and technology, between knowledge and security, between the archive and the weapons system. Verne's novel appeared at the foundational moment of modern logistics in war-fare, and it introduces a new and parallel logistics of the archive. The architectonics of museums and armies had long been related: in the eighteenth century, when standing armies occupied fortresses, museums resembled magazines; during the first half of the nine-teenth century, when the predatory tactics of Napoleon governed the conduct of war, museums became predators, often relying on armies for acquisitions (as in the case of the Elgin marbles) and often turning to tempestuous Napoleonic figures for leadership (as in the case of Panizzi). In the late Victorian period the logistics of the archive came to be marked by a system of continuous supply linking base with base, and bases with metropole. In 1871 the German forces under von Moltke invading France had constructed a compre-hensive system of supply that enabled them to overcome what Clausewitz had called the 'friction' of war, attaining a high mobility and realizing their maximum theoretical speed as determined by the technological means then available.[7] In a parallel way Verne's novel constructs a complete logistics of comprehensive knowledge. The archive gradually comes forward in the course of the novel in a variety of specifically modern logistical capacities and attributes. It appears as raw data, as classification systems able to absorb the artifacts of the material world into its own internal order, as arsenal, as military structures of rank and precedence, and most importantly, as the central chamber of a mobile and malleable new weapons system, the submarine. The novel takes the form of a series of incidents that foreground the fatal economy of force that inheres in the Victorian archive, and it places an archival logistics at the center of an invasion narrative that transforms the sea into the site of a new imperium.

Our initial impression is that Nemo's underwater empire consists solely of raw data. Fully half of the novel is devoted to listing phenomena observed. Though these inventories are often highly individuated (Aronnax tends to order things by sight, Ned by taste, Conseuil by taxonomy, Nemo by temporal sequence), Verne pre-sents them as unimpeachably positive knowledge. But the fact is that this raw data has already been, as statisticians say, 'cooked.' Un-awares, the archival gaze has combined the triple register of inquiry, measure and examination to prepare data to be acted upon by the variable modalities of power. The novel works to transform its central ideological project, the conquest of energy sources, into a phenomenology of the archival gaze trained on seemingly undifferentiated information presented at random. Verne never takes an inventory of anything that has clearly been manufactured by human beings; the novel includes no figures on the number of ballast tanks in the submarine, its maximum crew, its capacity for provisions. Instead Verne supplies us with lists of materials awaiting transformation. As formulated by Kelvin, the first law of thermodynamics posited that matter and energy can be transformed but not destroyed.[8] Verne very selectively interprets this law to mean that matter and energy exist in a state of latency awaiting a certain kind of productive transformation. Raw data, then, means raw materials. The inventoried contents of Nemo's ocean are a vision of an empire of energy sources, a combined mine and plantation that offers him an endless source of supply without confronting him with the labor troubles that usually plague mining conglomerates and cash-crop cartels. In *20,000 Leagues Under the Sea* the ocean is a depopulated Ceylon, Bolivia, South Africa, India.

The ordering frame within which Verne places raw but regulated data is the museum. The *Nautilus*'s on-board museum contains fixed glass cases displaying unusual specimens, rare paintings and manuscript scores, but the facility's most interesting feature is an observation deck which allows the observer to supplement the collection with an endless phenomenal procession of raw data. As at the Crystal Palace of the 1851 Great Exhibition, the wonder of the *Nautilus* museum is not its contents but the special effects devised to illuminate them. More than anything else, the museum equips the submarine with an aesthetic system for processing information. From the observation deck of the museum, Aronnax, himself a museum curator in Paris, practices a kind of underwater urbanism. He views the ocean as the *flâneur* views the street, continually experiencing the direct or indirect side effects of movement among moving bodies and objects. 'The scenery seemed to change for our own pleasure,' says Aronnax at one point.[9] This mobile museum furnishes him with rapid information – so rapid that it has not entered into or passed through the median stages of transmission or transportation set up by nineteenth-century technologies such as telegraph or freight. The motto of the *Nautilus*, 'mobilis in mobile,' perfectly expresses the new geostrategic capability of the museum to offer a continuous interface between words and things. That is to say, the museum constructs an imperceptible order in which perception (of things) and interpretation (via words) coincide in space and time.[10] In the *Nautilus* the museum has become what André Malraux would later call the 'museum without walls,' a space in which the ocean must be regarded as nothing more than a vast aquarium.

This same attention to the ubiquity of the archive recurs when Verne turns to the submarine and its paramilitary organization. Nemo's sailors wear uniforms and speak an artificial language that no one but a crew member can understand (a premonition of the closed speech of specialist jargon). Today's submarines, however, are weapons of pure war which can devastate continents, while Verne's *Nautilus* is an archival facility for capturing and processing data. Though torpedoes had long been imagined, Verne does not equip the *Nautilus* with them. He regards the submarine not as a war-machine but as an archive-machine. The distinction is crucial. To Verne, firepower is less important than knowledge-power, which consists not in destroying an object but in locating it and keeping it in constant sight as a target of knowledge. Nemo's continuous electro-optical surveillance of the sea (using Bunsen cells, Krupp engines and Rouquayrol diving apparatus) exhibits an archival construction of power based not on explosives and delivery systems but on the instant power of sensors, interceptors, and remote electronic detectors. His intention is to take aim along a given line of sight, to fix a subject of knowledge as an object of perception. He yearns to collect 'more accurate figures' (124). As much as possible Nemo refrains from participating in events, and he captivates Aronnax not with gymnastic coastguard rescues of sinking ships but with the idea of detailed observation without intervention, 'the idea of actually witnessing a sinking and, in a sense, being able to photograph its final moments' (128).[11] Nemo's *Nautilus* is not a gun but a camera, the forerunner not of modern ballistics (with its emphasis on payload and throw-weight) but of the very military analysis that superintends the automated perception of territory. Nemo and his submarine epitomize the moment in history when, as Merleau-Ponty has written, 'the problem of knowing who is the subject of the state and war [becomes] exactly the same kind as the problem of knowing who is the subject of perception.'[12]

Though Nemo assembles all the components of a perceptual logistics of warfare, he lacks one central feature identified by Merleau-Ponty: he is a perceiver without a state. It bothers Aronnax that Nemo does not submit his findings to any agency of state control, command or intelligence. Nemo has no juridical or political identity; in the eyes of the state, any state, he is a nonentity, legally nobody (as his name implies). Aronnax does not care to which state Nemo belongs. What matters is that Nemo does not designate the state as the necessary end result assigned to all social and technological development. Like most of Verne's characters, Aronnax subscribes to the most basic presupposition of the ideology of progress, namely, that progress means that history is a one-way progression toward the state.[13] In literary history the ship at sea had often served as a working model of civil society, the ship of state. But Aronnax simply does not understand that Nemo has assembled a working model not of civil society but of general diaspora. Nemo's procedures of appearance and disappearance have a prospective character for populations: his situation looks ahead to the governments in exile of the twentieth century, not just the temporarily dislocated 'Free French' directed by De Gaulle from his submarine during World War II (vividly realized in Pynchon's portrait of the Argentinian polity-as-submarine in *Gravity's Rainbow*), but the permanently dislocated polities dissolved into a state of precarious survival, the Poles in 1940s London, the ships of passportless Jews unable to dock anywhere in the Nazi-controlled Mediterranean. The forerunner of today's Palestinians, Nemo has no nationality but lives in the world at large. He is a legal inhabitant not of a specific territory but of the global media, which monitors his every move with great interest, treats his every action as the unfolding of a sensation novel, and acts as a kind of United Nations superintending the international police action that ends up depositing Aronnax on board the *Nautilus*. Watching the spectacle of the sea unfold from his protected position on the museum observation deck, Aronnax also regards Nemo as the undisputed master of a new kind of audiovisual empire. If in the nineteenth century Ratzel had claimed that 'war consists in extending one's frontiers across the boundaries of others,' one can say that Nemo has extended his in the form of information across the entire world.[14]

But this suppression of national frontiers, this hyper-communica-bility of information, does not succeed in enlarging the space of movement or in remaining external to the exercise of state power. Rather it signals the collapse and disappearance of the unknown and the unknowable before the expansion of a very tangible totalitarian power, an ever more refined and rapid technical control of compre-hensive knowledge, knowledge here not of the land but of the sea. For Nemo is not only a refugee but an invader. He does not invade the sea to pursue a political end, as Clausewitz said, 'by other means'; if he has an ideology (beyond the resolute positivism that actuates all Verne's characters), he refuses to articulate it. He abducts three Frenchmen without attempting to ransom them to the French government. And he entirely eschews the question that preoccupies most states, the question of legitimation. Rather than articulating strategy, he practices tactics, choosing to concentrate on perfecting a logistics for dominating the sea epistemologically. Like Phileas Fogg in *Around the World in Eighty Days* (1872), Nemo makes a global circuit, but unlike Fogg, his circuit aims at amassing comprehensive knowledge through invasion and occupation. All over the world Nemo sets up imperial institutions and channels of communication. He hunts fish in forests, excavates minerals in mines, establishes supply depots, measures depths and distances, speaks an administrative vernacular, even plants his flag to demar-cate territory. This recapitulation of state geographical prerogatives – what can be called an aquagraphy – can be seen most clearly in the chapter where the *Nautilus* passes through the underwater double to De Lesseps's Suez Canal. Considered at first to be a physical impossibility, the construction of the Suez Canal took fifteen years and involved forced labor, the use of dynamite, and a total expendi-ture of half a billion francs. The canal opened in 1869, but it took until 1888 for the major European powers to sign the Suez Canal Convention, which stipulated that the canal should 'always be free and open, in time of war as in time of peace, to every vessel of commerce or of war, without distinction of flag.'[15] Passing directly under the Suez Canal, Nemo becomes the state's liminal double: whether he likes it or not, his route striates the sea in tacit confor-mity with an order of movement ratified by international convention.

Nemo's archival construction of power, then, cannot be separated from his archival disposition of force. The novel opens as the *Nautilus* rams an American vessel under Commander Farragut, unfolds as the grand tour of an underwater empire, and records the experiences in captivity of its narrator, Aronnax. In essence the novel opens up a new space of armed conflict, the space of permanent undeclared war.[16] Undeclared war does not require a formal announcement of hostilities; because it has not been stated (quite literally, proclaimed by a state), it need not unfold over a given territory (Vietnams always shade into Cambodias); it does not even acknowledge a manifest enemy. With its nomadic submarine at war with the forces of land, *20,000 Leagues Under the Sea* is the foundational fiction of the archival logistics of permanent war, which is always the war not of actual but of utopian invasions. Heir to a long string of utopias, or nowheres, the narrative of Nemo, or nobody, performs an incredibly influential operation: it figures invasion as utopia, and utopia as the condition, place and situation of personal and political paranoia.

Published in the same year as Verne's novel, *The Battle of Dorking* deployed fictional scare tactics to a particular end: it explicitly agitates for the social and technological reform of armies and navies and culminates in a one-dimensional military ideology. In the 1870s such ideology led to the formation of modern propaganda (a propaganda which only its critics took at face value) and the invention of a variety of military traditions such as regimental colors, banners, histories, ties, and mascots. In *20,000 Leagues Under the Sea*, however, this cardboard ideology has become a utopian epistemology, a disposition to knowledge and a will to power oriented around the military-archival capabilities of a presumed enemy. In Verne's novel this enemy archive, based as it is on the compilation of comprehensive positive knowledge, still retains a certain neutrality; despite his dislike of captivity, Aronnax cannot help respecting Nemo's abilities as engineer, explorer and navigator. But only a thin line divides extraterritorial from extraterrestrial, utopia from dystopia. In the final analysis Nemo's invasion and occupation of the sea must be seen as a foundation not only of the invasion novel but of the divided invasion narratives of modern science fiction, which alternate between seeing interstellar invaders as belligerent (as in H.G. Wells's *The War of the Worlds* [1897]) and benign (as in Arthur C. Clarke's *Childhood's End* [1959]). Captain Nemo is the first in a long line of space invaders – quite literally, invaders of territorial space – who threaten to triumph because they control an archive of alien comprehensive knowledge.

Nemo, however, does not yet possess the capacity to produce panic or provoke general paranoia among the earth's populations.[17] In *20,000 Leagues* Nemo is more fearing than feared: he is the one who dreads invasion, and despite the techno-archival rationality of his underwater empire, his paranoia regarding the land and its products entirely lacks rationale (he disappears without ever justifying himself). The narrative of the all-powerful and all-knowing alien presupposes an actual alienation, a Manichean aesthetics demarcating a very real enemy capable of provoking a justifiable paranoia. In mid-twentieth-century America the representation of the UFO replicated the ideology of Cold War with the Soviet Union. In late nineteenth-century Britain such an enemy had yet to be delimited. It is often forgotten that alliances in the nineteenth century were in a state of continuous flux. The Triple Entente and Central Powers alliances were not formed until 1903, and as late as 1894 a war scare broke out over the French annexation of Madagascar. 'We spoke of nothing else,' wrote Somerset Maugham in his diary. 'There was a long discussion about the first movements of the war: we talked about what would happen if the French landed an army on the English coast; where they would land; what would be their movements; and how they would be prevented from taking London.'[18]

Like so many others, this scare took the form of a collective war game, an imagined violation of territory shared by an entire population and entailing the repeated superimposition of logistical grids over British territory. Though almost all late Victorian invasion narratives work within the logistical configuration invented by the German army, the invading armies always had something of the orientalism of the science-fiction invader about them (a lot of invasion narratives went so far as to feature polyglot mercenaries, pirates and mongol hoards). It would take until 1903 to bring these fictions into factual alignment with the archival capacity of an actual enemy who now emerged as the product of a stable configuration of alliances and counter-alliances. Aside from the project of comprehensive knowledge, Verne's Captain Nemo had lacked any overall plan or long-range design. In *The Riddle of the Sands* (1903), Erskine Childers better understood the crucial importance of the logistics of comprehensive knowledge. An admirer of Bismarck and von Moltke, Childers knew that the drive was on for a general system of intelligence that would allow everything to be seen and known, at every moment and in every place.

II

The Riddle of the Sands is a novel of what can be called thick geography. Childers follows the movements of two Englishmen holidaying on the North Sea coast of Germany who gradually document a German plan for the invasion of England, and he introduces a new logistics of perception into the archival reconnaissance of territory. Throughout history armies have tended to regard reconnaissance exclusively as a re-knowing, as a confirmation of the already known and knowable, as an epistemology without an attendant phenomenology. Early in the twentieth century Baden-Powell inadvertently revealed the low esteem in which reconnaissance was held by recruiting not adults but adolescents as scouts, and he trained them not to write maps but to read them (in *Scouting for Boys* [1908] he wrongly characterizes Kipling's Kim, a trained military geographer, as a 'scout'). Command centers have notoriously exhibited complete disregard of the various perceptual apparatuses at their disposal, particularly when these have produced information that conflicted with existing configurations of knowledge. The Light Brigade knew in advance about the Russian artillery crescent in the Crimea, Custer knew about the trap Sitting Bull had laid for him at the Little Big Horn, America knew about Pearl Harbor, the Nazis knew about D-Day. In *The Riddle of the Sands*, Davies, an amateur sailor, and Carruthers, a state functionary employed by the Foreign Office, successfully turn an intensely phenomenal perception of territory into a new kind of archival early-warning system. They wage a war not of projectiles but of perceptions, a war not of achieved knowledge but of approximate knowledge, a war not of strategy but of logistics. In *The Riddle of the Sands* the invasion novel both reaches maturity and undergoes mitosis: for it is not only the first spy novel (with its archetypal synthesis of the military and the police) but the first sustained narrative of what an American military strategist once called 'pure logistics.'

George Thorpe's *Pure Logistics* (1917) is a useful parallel text in several senses. In the nineteenth century the Swiss theoretician Baron Jomini had defined logistics as a subordinate discipline concerned with moving persons and materials, supplying depots, maintaining communications, and replacing personnel. According to Thorpe, however, logistics is what enables warfare, and he was the first to advance the thesis that all strategy and tactics devolve on logistics. In doing so he revived and extended the old metaphor of the military theater: 'Strategy is to war what plot is to the play; Tactics is represented by the role of the players; Logistics furnishes the stage management, accessories, and maintenance. The audience, thrilled by the action of the play and the art of the performers, overlooks all the cleverly hidden details of stage management.'[19] The great majority of invasion novels in the late nineteenth and early twentieth centuries restricted themselves to plotting at strategy or playing at tactics; like the first board games released in the 1870s, they came equipped with a certain number of pieces and a well-defined set of rules. With narratives driven by no military strategy to speak of, and battles won and lost without recourse to tactics, most invasion novels focus entirely on logistics, defined by Thorpe as the one element of theater at which the Victorians happened to excel, namely, 'stagecraft, with its elaborate settings, its mechanical accessories, and its complete efficiency.' For Thorpe, logistics is the nuts and bolts of war, and war is the assembly and deployment not simply of persons and materials, but of theater.

Childers, however, does not construct a Victorian spectacular theater like the observation deck Verne builds into the museum on board the *Nautilus*. Unlike Verne's novel or any other late Victorian invasion narrative, *The Riddle of the Sands* plots the appearance of a logistical stagecraft oriented around the perception, organization, and management of minute detail. Childers himself had experienced war exclusively as a series of logistical details; during the Boer War he was an artillery driver charged with moving pieces over long distances and caring for his horses. Throughout his novel the material world appears as a series of continually updated topographical references to a continually shifting terrain. In this novel every detail counts; much of the narrative comprises a detailed actuarial anatomy of sea, sand, wind, rain, and mud. It comes equipped with a series of maps to which Childers makes continual reference, establishing a continuous interlock between reading and orienteering (the art of 'taking a reading' using compass and map). As the narrative proceeds the scale of maps decreases, encouraging an even more precise dual reading. This graduated reading, however, does not lead to a major military action; no invasion or occupation takes place; no high-tech instruments take center stage. Instead the novel's combatants wage an undeclared war of nerves, quite literally a neurasthenic war of nervous susceptibility to a changing environment. Freud later defined war neurosis as the interpretation of all phenomena, especially ordinary details from everyday life, as signs of war (the movement of a bird in a bush might for example be taken for a sniper taking aim). In *The Riddle of the Sands* Davies and Carruthers display the features of a prewar neurosis in which the phenomenology of perception leads directly to an awareness of the insecurity of territory, to a recognition of the imbalance of power and, most of all, to the detection of the animating presence of an enemy archive, watching, recording, waiting.

Preoccupied with an extensive anatomy of a little-known segment of the German North Sea coast, the novel reproduces the fundamental tenet of all military geography: that every feature of the visible world possesses actual or potential military significance. The novel begins as Carruthers purchases surveying instruments at a London warehouse. When he arrives in Flensburg, Davies gives him a lecture in military geography, calling attention to the strategic importance of Germany's 120 miles of coast. 'Compare that with the seaboard of France and England. Doesn't it stand to reason that every inch of it is important?'[20] Over and over again the novel unapologetically takes the lay of the coast. 'I make no apology for having described these early days in some detail. . . . For every trifle, sordid or picturesque, was relevant; every scrap of talk a link; every passing mood critical for good or ill' (73). Most of the work Davies and Carruthers perform aboard the *Dulcibella* is archival work, and the novel consists largely of an archival record culminating in their discovery of a German plan for invading England. But whereas Nemo's archival work always took place in great proximity to an archival facility, and combined both theoretical and practical components, their archival work is fully invested in its field of application and does not require the presence of a museum. 'There are too many of them,' says Davies of the naval books he keeps on board. 'Let's throw them overboard. They're very old anyhow, and I know them by heart' (152). *The Riddle of the Sands* is an anatomy of the archival gaze, an archival 'way of seeing' (76) fully invested in its field of vision, a mobile form of archivization that can do without an archive. Though at first they do not suspect that comprehensive enemy plans underlie the geographical knowledge they so comprehensively catalogue, as geographers they nevertheless proceed consistently under a hypothesis of design which assumes that all particulars are laden with generality, that all phenomena are epiphenomenal, that all accidence is the product of design.

The design that governs the apparent organization of the phenomenal world in *The Riddle of the Sands* has been derived from the master text of late nineteenth-century geography, Alfred Thayer Mahan's *The Influence of Sea Power Upon History* (1890). Davies makes continual reference to 'the much-thumbed pages' (69) of this 'ABC' (119) book, and it occupies a central position in the small 'library' (207) which the *Dulcibella*, like the *Nautilus*, contains. In the late nineteenth century, geography was the last empiricism, and Mahan's military geography was perhaps the ultimate empiricism, dividing the sea into a grid of traffic patterns. 'The sea presents itself,' writes Mahan, as 'a great highway; or better, perhaps, [as] a wide common, over which men may pass in all directions, but on which some well-worn paths show that controlling reasons have led them to choose certain lines of travel rather than others' (25). Captain Nemo had taken a step in this direction by carrying out most of his operations on the sea floor, on underwater land. Mahan goes one step further and treats the surface of the sea as if it were land. He sees the sea, a fairly empty space, as a system of passages such as highways, canals, trade routes. Mahan's essential contribution to geography was that he read history as a sequence of great naval battles 'less determined by the shrewdness and foresight of governments than by conditions of position, extent, number and character of . . . natural conditions' (28) – fixed conditions which the geographer actively helps to construct and impose on the space of the sea.

The Riddle of the Sands replicates the ideology of Mahan's theory
of history even as it deconstructs his empirical constitution of sea
space. Mahan provides the text and pretext for Davies's conviction
that 'we're a maritime nation – we've grown by the sea and live by it;
if we lose command of it we starve' (119). For Mahan, commanding
the sea means treating it as a Cartesian grid. His illustrations all
show neat rows of ships moving across a flat and uniform space
conducive to command – a kind of parking lot for ships. This open
sea differs drastically from the closed sea that fascinates Childers. As
a naval geographer Mahan views land and sea as complementary
mirror images, each structured according to a system of regularities,
each composed of a distinct element (earth or water). Childers,
however, directs his attention at the narrow and shifting front that
divides and connects land and sea. He sets his novel along a segment
of the German coast renowned for its ambiguity. There 'the islands
and coasts are scarcely visible, they are so low, and everything looks
the same' (61). In front of Carruthers's very eyes 'the whole face of
the waters was changing from moment to moment' (128). Land
becomes sea and sea becomes land. From the outset the focus is on
intensive rather than extensive space, on tactile rather than visual
qualities, on a disjunctive rather than a conjunctive perception of
territory. This is the kind of space that turns all fixed positions into
sand castles: 'I waited on deck and watched the death-throes of the
suffocating sands under the relentless onslaught of the sea. The last
strongholds were battered, stormed, and overwhelmed; the tumult
of sounds sank and steadied, and the sea swept victoriously over the
whole expanse' (134).

Neither sea nor land, this constantly shifting terrain registers the
growing derealization of the confident archival gaze of Mahan and
other late Victorian geographers. In *The Riddle of the Sands* maps
obliterate rather than indicate position, impede rather than facili-
tate movement. Meditating on 'the prehistoric rottenness of the
English charts' (96), Childers can often sound like his contemporary, Saussure: 'The strokes, of course, are only conventional signs,
and do not correspond in the least to individual "booms," which are
far too numerous and complex to be indicated accurately on a chart,
even of the largest scale. The same applies to the channels themselves
whose minor meanderings cannot be reproduced' (130). Even the
act of taking bearings causes vertigo: 'Any attempt at orientation

made me giddy' (196). In this world of highly artificial representations not even the language of the geographer suffices to give the
reader a clear idea of where Davies and Carruthers are at any given
moment. Terrain was 'becoming unintelligible; clean-cut coasts and
neat regiments of little figures have given place to a confusion of
winding and intersecting lines and bald spaces' (60). Throughout the
novel Childers must supply his readers with maps to which his
narrator, who is often lost himself, makes continual reference. These
appended maps are highly approximate constructions; one warns of
'sands continually changing,' while another, 'a rough sketch of the
scene as I partly saw and chiefly imagined it,' is little more, as
Carruthers freely admits, than a 'mental photograph' (237) taken in
the dark. Here, as elsewhere, Childers summons up the power of
geography as a science of imaginary precision able to produce
representations that exist without certain reference to anything at
all. In this novel maps have lost their use-value, just as they did later
during the First World War when artillery constantly turned the
terrain upside down and removed the topographical references
crucial to the organization of battle.

Davies and Carruthers soon recognize that the very liminality of
the land–sea interface poses a major security risk within their
empirical regime of geographical knowledge. In military theory and
practice, the threshold between land and sea is the meeting-ground
for many vectors of force, and the site of much uncertainty; for every
D-Day there has been a Dunkirk, a Gallipoli, or a Bay of Pigs. In *The
Riddle of the Sands* the two sailors find it increasingly difficult to
update their picture of reality. They regularly confront not hard but
soft facts. To align perception along an imaginary axis, Davies and
Carruthers employ a succession of models to explain the fragmented
data that comes their way. In rapid succession they advance and
disprove a 'channel theory,' a 'mushroom theory,' and a 'Memmert
theory.' Each of these theories assumes that the Germans are acting
defensively, preparing fortifications, reinforcing dikes, constructing
submarine pens. Each assumes that the Germans are attempting to
dominate the sea by dominating privileged places on land overlook-
ing the sea. Most of all, each appeals to them primarily because it
stabilizes the phenomena at hand. In this novel the visible world
passes before their eyes once, and once only. Within the liminal zone
of the shifting sands, any recurring mark or feature carries with it an

aura of certainty (Davies convinces Carruthers of the seriousness of his purpose by managing to retrace his path across the volatile waters of the Juist strand). From the beginning of the novel until nearly its end, Childers treats these fact-building theories as hallucinations of order amidst the hallucinatory disorder of land and sea, where, as Davies and Carruthers exhaust theory after theory, their 'demoralized library' (198) becomes less and less able to assert and maintain the order of things.

The peculiar genius of the German invasion plan lies precisely in its ability to attract and repel the empiricities of the inquiring geographical gaze. 'From first to last circumstances drove us deeper and deeper into the wrong groove, till the idea became inveterate that the secret we were seeking was one of defence and not offence' (305). The plan depends upon a crucial inversion: in essence it turns territory inside out by setting up a system of canals deep inside Germany that serve as bases for assembling an inland fleet. 'Orthodox invasions,' explains Carruthers, 'start from big ports and involve a big fleet of ocean transports' (305). The German plan calls for improving, deepening, and canalizing seven minor streams that lead to the German coast; for converting coal barges into ocean-going troop carriers; for drawing on the natural camouflage of the coast; and for placing the whole operation not under military command but under the dispersed supervision of a group of commercial investors. A masterpiece of means and ends, the German plan depends for its success on the central tenet of modern logistics: that political economy become indistinguishable from the economy of war. Davies and Carruthers have their suspicions, but they always direct them at particular objects. Only at the very end of the novel do they realize that *everything they have seen* belongs to an economy of pure war coextensive with Germany itself.

The core of the plan involves the construction and extension of canals. Davies and Carruthers travel back and forth on the new Kaiser Wilhelm Canal without in the least suspecting that it forms the grand trunk road for the coming invasion of England. Carruthers knows perfectly well that the canal is 'a symbol of the new and mighty force which, controlled by the genius of statesmen and engineers, is thrusting the empire irresistibly forward to the goal of maritime greatness' (117). This equation of statesmen and engineers is crucial. In *A Thousand Plateaus* (1980) Deleuze and Guattari have seen waterworks as the basic signature of the imperial state: 'the State needs to subordinate hydraulic force to conduits, pipes, embankments, which prevent turbulence, which constrain movement to go from one point to another, and space itself to be striated and measured, which makes the fluid dependent on the solid, and flows proceed by parallel, laminar layers.'[21] Throughout history, states aspiring to imperial status have tended to regulate the overland flow of water: through aqueducts (in ancient Rome), city canals (in late medieval Venice), dikes (in the sixteenth-century Dutch Confederation), isthmus canals (in Victorian Egypt and Panama), or through filters and additives (in twentieth-century America). This hydraulic striation of terrain defines what we now call 'public works,' and the real genius of the German plan is that it transforms a static and ordinal system of ducts into a flexible and heterogeneous series of passages into enemy territory. Secrecy resides best in paradox, and the paradox of the German waterworks is that they are a fixed means for facilitating flow, an immobile technology for assisting movement, a public system of embankments capable of concealing a top-secret undertaking on a vast scale. The plan also exploits the fact that, to the late nineteenth-century imagination, canals were ventures of empire, slender threads linking one exotic place with another, as in Panama or Egypt. In *The Riddle of the Sands* the German Navy means to transform a public network of canals – one of the nation's major means of mass transportation – into a field of force. The military secret has become a collective secret integrated into the conduct of everyday civilian life, and the German high command's secret weapon has become not high technology, with its cadres of specialists and lexicon of jargon, but low technology basic to the existence of an entire population.[22]

That Davies and Carruthers ultimately solve the riddle of the sands derives only in part from internal defects in the German plan. Without question a canal is a narrow windpipe through which it is difficult for an armed body to draw air. When the *Dulcibella* passes through Holland, where canal movement has been perfected as nowhere else, Davies considers it 'a wretched business, nothing but paying lock-dues, bumping against schuyts, and towing down stinking canals' (59). Canals make movement dependent upon single concentrated lines of supply, fixed, visible, permanent, open to sabotage. But Davies and Carruthers do not succeed in foiling the

German plan by attempting sabotage; this would be to act against another state, and to upset the very balance of knowledge and power which, as amateur spies and state servants, they are trying to preserve (in both war and peace states tend to respect one another's waterworks, and correspondingly, the destruction of large-scale waterworks tends to be an anarchist act, as in Edward Abbey's *The Monkey Wrench Gang* [1974]).[23] Their success can rather be understood as a result of a logistics of knowledge that they improvise to comprehend a shifting and derealized perceptual field. The novel chronicles their adjustment to an asymmetrical perceptual field in which obligatory reference points have been obliterated, and it traces the process by which they devise highly versatile modes of counter-perception to match and surpass the Germans at their own ambulant game.

The first half of the novel is a detailed record of events that explode the homogeneity of the geographical gaze and replace it with a heterogeneity of perceptual fields. Much of the movement here takes place under classic battlefield conditions. The weather is bad, the terrain is unreliable, and most importantly, visibility is limited. Davies and Carruthers cannot physically see their position and so have to rely on map coordinates (with miserable results, as shown). Under such conditions know-how gradually gives way to feel-how, and a different patterning of the human sensorium emerges. Deprived of prosthetic implements for extending and heightening vision, Davies, the more experienced sailor of the two, has to resort to touch, reflex, sound, smell. 'I believe,' Carruthers marvels, 'he could *smell* sand where he could not see or touch it' (143). Like Kipling's Mowgli he slows down his movement in order to speed up the pace of his perception. 'I don't go in for speed' (195), says Davies, who at one point reprimands Carruthers for having 'rushed over that last part like an express train' (63). A military buff, Davies seems well aware of the constraints that newly devised forms of high speed have placed on movement and perception. To use Davies's example, rail transportation provided nineteenth-century armies with a new speed of movement, but without an accompanying flexibility; just as armies could now outpace their lines of supply, the speed of movement could now run well ahead of the human capacity to absorb information. Under such conditions knowledge barely exists, for machines must take over the functions of monitoring and assimilating knowledge. To retain the maneuverability of his senses, and to recover the possibility of an epistemology of reconnaissance, Davies has to renounce high technology and mobilize a logistics of obsolescence.[24]

The maritime idiom of the novel, perhaps its most celebrated feature, results directly from Davies's systematic use of low technology as an effective form of twentieth-century reconnaissance. The novel's unparalleled density of nautical detail consists largely of an anatomy of the *Dulcibella*'s 'plain domestic economy' (147) in which 'the whole fun of the thing is to do everything oneself' (54). As equipment the *Dulcibella* is a specimen of derelict technology; 'in the distant past she had been a lifeboat, and had been clumsily converted into a yacht by the addition of a counter, deck, and the necessary spars. She was built, as all lifeboats are, diagonally, of two skins of teak, and this had immense strength, though, in the matter of looks, all a hybrid's failings' (49). This foregrounding of conventional technology has no parallel in previous invasion novels, most of which began and ended as ballistics exercises structured around one question: what new weapons would have a decisive effect on the next war? In *Anticipations* (1902), H.G. Wells had written that 'war is being drawn into the field of the exact sciences. Every additional weapon, every new complication of the art of war, intensifies the need of deliberate preparation, and darkens the outlook of a nation of amateurs.'[25] In a crucial ideological move *The Riddle of the Sands* reverses Wells's position: in this novel the process of technological extrapolation and modification, the construction of new and improved models of dreadnought-class battleships, does not give England or any other country a leading edge. The logic of the Victorian arms race had based military preparedness on technological sophistication. Childers, however, thinks of military preparedness as contingent upon a regression in basic technology. No mere alarmist, he advances a mythology of the demilitarized war economy, that is, the myth of a society capable of maintaining a permanent war footing without mortgaging its surplus to a military-industrial complex, and without resorting to the applied force of the security state.

The German invasion plan had also depended on basic technologies, but the English response envisioned by Childers differs from it in several important respects. The German plan incorporates state-run technologies of movement into a military infrastructure; it entails the takeover of one dominant technology of power by another, which preserves it intact and puts it to different uses. Whereas the German plan transfers power between complementary and symmetrical modalities of dominant knowledge (a quintessential twentieth-century coup d'état in which the state gives way to the military), Childers's scheme of English response locates power in sets of low-ranking knowledges, dominated knowledges, disqualified knowledges outside the purview of the state and beneath the contempt of the dominant. This is local knowledge, differential knowledge dispersed regionally, forgotten or barely remembered at the centers of power, a folkloric archive preserved by eccentrics like Davies. 'There must be hundreds like me – I know a good many myself – who know our coasts like a book' (119). Davies dreams of an English resistance based upon what Foucault has called 'a reactivation of local knowledges – of minor knowledges, as Deleuze might call them – in opposition to the scientific hierarchization of knowledges and the effects intrinsic to their power.'[26] His plan to resist the German invasion entails a national insurrection of local knowledges, and it owes its force not only to the fatal regularity of the German plan, which is after all an exercise in siegecraft, but to the very irregularity of local knowledge itself: 'The millions we sink in forts and mines won't carry us far. They're fixed – pure passive defence. What you want is *boats* – mosquitos with stings – swarms of them – patrol-boats, scout-boats, torpedo-boats; intelligent irregulars manned by local men, with a pretty free hand to play their own game. And what a game to play!' (145)

In *The Riddle of the Sands*, then, the defense of England resides in an arsenal of hobbies. Carruthers returns again and again to his description of Davies as 'an enthusiast with hobbies' (105), and with good reason. In nineteenth-century Britain hobbies were the graveyard for subjugated knowledges and superseded technologies. Think of gardens preserving the uses of implements long outmoded on farms, yachts preserving the knowledge of wind-driven transportation, toy soldiers preserving the massed formations of land wars long after Britain stopped fighting France on the Continent, scholars preserving dead or nearly dead languages like Old English or Gaelic.

In other European countries during the nineteenth century, the great emblems of popular defense were common tools and artifacts transformed from ordinary usage – caps, hammers, sickles, hunting equipment, armbands, bricks (used in erecting barricades).[27] Though Britain never experienced the equivalent of 1848 or 1871, Childers reproduces the essential semiosis of a group coalescing around the defense of its place of habitation. But whereas on the Continent these tools and weapons signified opposition to an existing state, for Childers they signify adherence to one. To counter the onslaught of the destructive systems brought forward by the German military machine, Childers invents a form of popular defense in which regional and marginal knowledges could conceivably form the first line of state defense. Like other Edwardian figurations of the hobbyist-hero preparing for war (most notably Baden-Powell's *Scouting for Boys*), *The Riddle of the Sands* predicted a more mobile war than actually took place. Unlike them, however, it foresaw a conflict in which victory would be founded only on the degree to which all forms of civilian activity, even those in which the state takes little or no formal or official interest, could be integrated into a single system of civil defense.

Davies's plan for the mobilization of local knowledge as defense, however, does not entirely explain his own peculiar status as an informal state operative. He does not hold a state position and he views state functionaries with contempt: 'those Admiralty chaps want waking up' (108). The state he serves is neither *de jure* nor *de facto*; rather he has in mind a kind of state-in-process which asserts its dominance through nonhegemonic modes of cognition. For Davies, the state is not a matter of presence or absence, of wholes or nothings, of internals or externals, of geographies versus blank spaces on the map. The power of the state, rather, resides in difference, in what Deleuze and Guattari call a 'nonlimited locality' (383) of local operations, in a lack both of objects and objectives. 'Of our destination and our objects, if we had any, I knew nothing' (74). What Carruthers calls 'the casual character of our adventure' (114) unfolds on 'a desert of sand' (131) over which Davies moves as 'the street arab who zigzags under the horses' feet unscathed' (113). This objectless surveillance is not spying – 'I don't think spy is the right word' (94) says Davies at one point – but what has been called state nomodology, or the integration of disintegration into a network of designs sanctioned by the state.

Later perfected by T.E. Lawrence, the work of the state nomad does not unfold in relation to a centered structure or a fixed orientation. It relies not on a unified field theory of power but on a diversity of fields of applied knowledge. Nevertheless it presupposes a teleology of information and relies on certain mechanisms for insuring that the power embodied in knowledge resides finally, and securely, with the state. State nomads do not necessarily work for the state or even reside in it (in Childers's novel Davies never enters England), but they are adept at working out complex lines of alliance and affiliation for transferring intelligence to the state. In *The Riddle of the Sands* this transference pairs Davies with Carruthers, a low-level Foreign Office functionary. A dandy of sorts, Carruthers has hitherto experienced yachting not as a dominated but as a dominant knowledge, as the conspicuous consumption of luxury. When he joins Davies in Germany he reveals what a struggle it is for the dominant to know what they have dominated: as Davies teaches him the 'tactics' of low-tech sailing, he 'struggled to apprehend, careless for the moment as to whether they were worth knowing, but doggedly set on knowing them' (74). The point at which Carruthers apprehends the value of this dominated knowledge is the point at which he takes control of the novel's narrative. In the first half of the novel Carruthers records Davies's monologues on Mahan and assimilates his instructions for operating the *Dulcibella*; in the second half Carruthers no longer needs Davies to carry out the functions of control, command and communication, and he reduces him to the status of his personal pilot and navigator (like Nemo, Davies is a geophobe who does not function well on dry land). For all his local knowledge, Davies's knowledge is merely local, and he persists to the end in believing that the Germans are undertaking some sort of localized defensive action (this theory 'had become a sort of religion with him' [216]). By the beginning of the eighteenth chapter Davies has become dispensable, and the narrative has transferred the burden of proof from the naive and intuitive phenomenology of Davies to the ratiocinative state phenomenology of Carruthers.

The narrative registers Carruthers's ongoing archivization of local knowledge in a variety of ways. For Davies, power resides exclusively in the limited technology that he knows so well. As a state functionary, however, Carruthers knows how to amass and coordinate different technologies of power. Unlike Davies, who claims that 'there's really very little to tell' (58), he recognizes first that power resides in the administrative medium of narrative. Carruthers does the narrating and, by definition, the ordering of a narrative that moves from the sea toward its resolution on dry land. The novel relegates almost all land movement to Carruthers; on land he does most of the talking, the thinking, the listening, the theorizing. At sea Carruthers is at sea, having 'lost all idea of time and space, and felt like a senseless marionette kicking and jerking to a mad music without tune or time' (229). On land, however, he can transform this puppet show into a well-choreographed scene of late Victorian parlor drama in which, for the only time in the novel, he confronts all of his adversaries face to face. 'We had drifted into a ridiculous situation, and were like characters in one of those tiresome plays where misunderstandings are manufactured and so carefully sustained that the audience are too bored to wait for the denouement' (180). Displaying his mastery of the logistics of war as pure theater (as Thorpe predicted, war has become a matter of what the chapter title calls 'finesse'), Carruthers augments local knowledge gleaned from Davies with the cultural capital he possesses by virtue of his position as a bored state functionary. Only as Carruthers combines these twin technologies of power, placing local knowledge within a global economy, augmenting low technology with high culture, does the disintegrated geography of the sands gradually give way to an integrated picture of the planned German invasion.

This integrated picture, however, does not include a detailed account of the archival capacity of the presumed enemy. A riddle of the sands is both a riddle that can be solved and a geography that can be mastered; the riddle of the enemy poses a different kind of epistemological conundrum.[28] 'They,' Carruthers asks. 'Who are "they"? Who are our adversaries?' (111) This is no mere rhetorical question, for though Carruthers succeeds in exposing the invasion plan, the identity of his major adversary, Dollmann, remains a cipher. Even the Germans 'know very little of Herr Dollmann, of his origins, his antecedents' (175), and like Shakespeare's Iago he exits without ever explaining himself. In Dollmann the riddle of the sands becomes an enigma. As the name of the World War II intelligence project implies, an enigma is a state coding system so complex that it can only be broken by another state. In *The Riddle of the Sands* Childers sees all enigmas as issuing from state agency and agencies (only later in the twentieth century will novelists relegate figures like Dollmann to membership in independent crime polities such as Ian Fleming's 'Smersh'). The man's name evokes a doll manipulated by distant interests who manage to evade detection despite all setbacks. Unlike the riddle of the sands, the enigma of Dollmann can never be fully decoded, and the 'shock of enlightenment' (121) Carruthers experiences as a result of his outing with Davies extends only to the disturbing knowledge that Dollmann, the Germans' own version of a state nomad, was actually an Englishman. In a world where the balance of power depends on securing the uniform allegiance of subjects to the state, the defection of even a single self stands as a critical breach in the phalanx of national security. The environment of 'fancied security' (269) to which Carruthers belongs at the novel's outset finally gives way at the novel's conclusion to an environment of paranoia, a quintessentially jingoistic perception of potential disequilibrium in an international economy of balanced power.

The paranoid environment of *The Riddle of the Sands*, however, does not merely duplicate the alarmism of late Victorian imperial ideology. Much of the novel's paranoia turns on the complete control over information systems that Davies and Carruthers assume the Germans possess. Though they begin with the ordinary assumption that they can increase their power over the Germans by consuming knowledge about them, over time they come to the recognition that the knowledge they have consumed is power that has already been produced and distributed by the Germans themselves. Davies and Carruthers become paranoid when they realize that, far from being the putative basis of the empirical world, facts are factitious, malleable, objects of power and subject to control. The more they know, then, the less they know. Often the two suspect that they are the victims of a simulated flux, a state of indeterminacy directed by an enemy who contrives 'to gain knowledge and control of our movements' (183). Such interfacing of knowledge and control goes far beyond conventional attempts to turn geography to military advantage.[29] It is relatively easy to scramble geographical sign systems by forcing opponents to use old representations of territory (as when Davies and Carruthers have to rely on old charts), or even to strip territory of signs (as when Russians invading Czechoslovakia in 1968 discovered that all the road signs had been removed). Childers has in mind a far more comprehensive interrogation of phenomena. In *The Riddle of the Sands*, everything – all forms of narrative, all verbal utterances, all gestural communication, all geography and all aquagraphy – must be interrogated for complicity with hidden strategies of control. Childers attempts to shorten this list by asserting that 'facts are facts' (327), a statement which sounds comfortably empirical but which also stands as an emblem of the tautological character of information. In the last paragraph Childers has to admit that he does not know what other plans may exist in what he has called the 'German archives' (280). 'Others may be conceived,' he ends, allowing the interrogation of the visible world for enemy designs to expand beyond the temporal boundaries of his own narrative.

The last great hope of England, as well as the first line of defense against the enemy's archival capacity to constitute an environment, is the formation of a specifically corporate form of subjectivity. Corporate subjectivity must not be equated with the production of a uniform subjectivity fostered by the collective paranoia of late-Victorian jingoism, or later, of German fascism. Childers recognizes that the corporate subject is much more than a 'meddlesome alarmist' (121). Corporate subjectivity allows considerable room for difference, variation, replenishment and renewal. The corporate subject displays all the usual features of individuated bourgeois subjectivity, differing only in that it constitutes itself primarily, though not exclusively, in relation to a state. In *The Riddle of the Sands* selves tend initially to be individuated by eccentric practices that have possible centric military uses to the state, such as hobbies. Carruthers and Davies may despise Dollmann for being a marionette controlled by an enemy, but both are equally bound by invisible but irremediably prior ties to their own state, ties that often reveal state affiliation in unexpected ways. Whenever Davies tries to describe his romantic attachment to Dollmann's daughter he begins to speak officialese; he calls asking after her 'a private supplementary inquiry,' and even Carruthers, himself a state functionary, has to admit 'that's a long name to call it' (125). For his own part,

Carruthers frequently loses himself in 'reveries of things, not persons; of vast national issues rather than the poignant human interests so closely linked with them' (305). As a narrator he violates most of the conventions of the late Victorian novel when at the very end he abruptly refuses to divulge 'personal history,' which he maintains 'is of no concern to the outside world' (318). Childers views his characters as actors on an international stage, and individual subjectivity as case histories bearing on the selection and disposition of larger patterns of corporate activity. Like Kipling, who gives his state nomads numbers instead of names, or T.E. Lawrence, who changed his name several times to reassert his anonymity as a state servant, Childers consistently returns to the position that underneath it all, nationality, and nationality alone, constitutes the fundamental form of identity, a corporate identity predicated on 'the essential facts' of state hegemony, 'stripped of their warm human envelope' (18).

The great desideratum of the corporate subject is to attain an equilibrium of pressure between the collective paranoia sanctioned by the state and the individual paranoia experienced by the self. More than anything else, the corporate subject yearns to equalize the inner and outer pressures that operates on it. In *The Riddle of the Sands*, the coming invasion becomes not only a passive object of fear but also an active object of desire, for when the invasion comes, the worst will have happened and the corporate subject will finally be free from sudden changes of pressure; the state and the self will have reached full accommodation. At times Davies can barely contain his enthusiasm for the coming war. 'Germany's a thundering great nation,' he said; 'I wonder if we shall ever fight her' (68). The mere sight of warships prompts him to murmur 'ecstatically' (113). Like Cornelius Ryan's *The Longest Day* (1959), *The Riddle of the Sands* tells the story of an invasion awaited for so long that it has become a utopian project. By the end of the novel the coming invasion has become a utopian space of civil dislocation in which the very notion of what constitutes a boundary – not only the conventional boundary separating state and self but also the system of boundaries dividing geographical space – has undergone complete transformation.

Here it should be recalled that the invasion novel entered the field of discourse just as the layout of London no longer corresponded to the old division between the city and the country. In many Edwardian invasion narratives the battles take place almost exclusively in suburbs at the urban fringe. Childers's novel develops and extends this deconstruction of the urban layout in a variety of ways. In *The Riddle of the Sands*, as in earlier invasion narratives, the invasion is a utopia that cannot be enclosed within the perimeters of city walls. A utopian invasion is not a place of occupation but a vector of movement. It is almost never directed at occupying a sedentary urban space. Instead it bypasses cities or destroys them entirely. Davies voices a typical sentiment when he says, 'I hate towns' (67). In invasion novels the only surviving metropolis is the army. As an army the city no longer occupies a given piece of ground, but has become a polis-in-motion. In the military, strategists had long likened moving a large army to moving a city (in the nineteenth century logistics introduced and perfected the first means of mass transportation, and civilian authorities came to depend on advances in military logistics to supply them with basic technology). In the invasion novel, the army replaces the city as the locus of state power shifts from a territorial center, or metropolis, to an extraterritorial periphery lacking fixed geographical position. If the central figure of the invasion narrative is the state nomad, the capital city of the invasion narrative is the army encampment, the nebulous conurbation where the very technologies designed for the utmost speed and flexibility of movement serve as the basis for a military occupation.

The foundational fictions of the imperial archive had all imagined placing the military's field of operations at great remove from the metropole. Verne and Wells directed military technology at the moon, Hilton placed an archive-state in Tibet, and even Kipling, who dealt so vividly with barracks life in India, restricted himself to country scenes and public schools whenever he turned to metropolitan life. Within the imperial archive, the separation of Kipling's fiction into distinct zones of central and peripheral activity is exemplary. The archival construction of power perfected in mid-Victorian England had depended on a geopolitical separation of coercion and force. The use of coercion ruled at the metropole, enshrined in the activities of the police, while the use of force was relegated to the colonies, where armies were stationed. The achievement of the invasion novel was that it shattered the inviolability of the metropolis and figured a society in which the military and the police would increasingly share the same roles and inhabit a common space of representation. This is the space of national security, and Erskine Childers was among the first to see that it would be possible for war to be characterized as what Carruthers calls 'police duty' (176). What *The Riddle of the Sands* documents better than any turn-of-the-century narrative is the establishment of a mutual service pact between the military and the police. In later years the spy novel perfected the terms of the alliance, but already, in Childers's novel, it is no longer possible to locate distinct domains of civil and military activity. After the First World War the idea of the imperial archive lost its civilian coloration, and after the Second it lost even its stable national identity. The last section of this chapter will show that in the wartime London depicted in Pynchon's *Gravity's Rainbow*, the idea of the enemy archive also depends on the mutual development of military techniques of war and police techniques of surveillance. The production of war and the production of knowledge finally merged to form one common enterprise.

III

In the days and weeks before the Normandy invasion of June 1944, the Allied Supreme Command moved uneasily into a hermeneutic trance. It was a time of extraordinary epistemological density, when the daily routine of observation and counter-observation that occupied military intelligence on both sides of the English Channel pivoted on the divination of minutiae. The Allied armies had massed but the Germans did not know when and where they would strike. As D-Day approached, every feature of the phenomenal world was interrogated as a sign of the armies to come. British coastal radar reported on the flights of birds. German intelligence experts listened to BBC broadcasts of Paul Verlaine's poetry, hoping to locate passages that would mean something to the French Resistance. MI5 detained and interrogated the *Daily Telegraph*'s crossword-puzzle writer because he included a large number of highly confidential code words in the puzzle for June 2.[30] Up to the last minute Eisenhower surrounded himself with meteorologists who read the sky like court astronomers. It seemed that the epidermis of the war machine had peeled away to reveal a military mysticism obsessed with small signs, chance tokens, hidden correspondences, unfore-seen alignments of circumstance. All signs were potential omens, and all interpretation was a form of panic, for behind every reading there lay the possibility of an enemy writing.

The paranormal preoccupations of the Allied high command during Operation Overlord were the leading edge of a new military epistemology that had been long in the making. Magic epistemology returns information to knowledge, giving facts binding force only by desperate recourse to magic. In an age overwhelmed by information, magic is epistemology's last resort, offering the promise of the unity of knowledge. Astonishingly, however, this magic often turns out to be viable. The strangest and most influential text to come out of the First World War, T.E. Lawrence's *Seven Pillars of Wisdom* (1926), had been an unstable compound of military geography and oriental-ist mysticism. Lawrence was the first to move outside of the nineteenth-century equation of military intelligence with geography. The information he provided to the Foreign Office often appeared to him in visions, yet it proved reliable enough to dictate policy in the region.[31] The geography in which Lawrence had been schooled as a British Museum functionary was the lingua franca of the imperial archive at both metropole and colony, and in Kipling's *Kim* (1901) as in Childers's *The Riddle of the Sands*, the head of British Intelligence takes it for granted that the discipline defines the parameters of positive military knowledge. After the First World War geography lost its central position as new constructions of sense perception supplanted the solid positivities of geographical time and space. These constructions of control were highly volatile combina-tions of rational and irrational elements. The strange shape of Lawrence's narrative, with its striking juxtapositions of air warfare with nomadism, of prophecy with prudent statesmanship, points to a new magic epistemology in which intelligence could take as its domain not just what could be said, written and enumerated in catalogue form, but what could not be said, what was unsayable, unwritable, even unthinkable. The new magic epistemology sought out the edges of enunciation where the normal and normative shaded into the paranormal and parapositive. The production of war began to include the production of the vastly differentiated systems of knowledge that Foucault has in mind when he speaks of the archive as 'that which differentiates discourses in their multiple functioning.'[32]

The narrative of Pynchon's *Gravity's Rainbow* reproduces the highly differentiated archive of the Second World War. For, more than any previous conflict, the Second World War was a war of archives entailing a massive material, technical, and instrumental investment in knowledge. Like a comic strip character, SHAEF's (Supreme Headquarters of the Allied Expeditionary Forces) brain dwarfed its body, with the result that nearly seventy agencies were separately charged with gathering and codifying intelligence.[33] Pynchon takes as his starting point the play of the formal structures, points of contact, places of insertion and areas of operation that characterized different types of social knowledge in time of war. In Pynchon's novel the military does not occupy a distinct or homogeneous space of discourse. The army acronyms in which the book abounds define at best a limited space of communication. Every top-heavy bureaucracy in the novel leaves a waste trail of discarded languages: Kazakh, Herero, Hebrew, Argentine Spanish. A whole mass of knowledges – not just centric knowledges like cinematography, ballistics, statistics, chemistry and Pavlovian psychology, but eccentric knowledges like astrology, black magic, freemasonry and folktales – intrudes to widen radically the general epistemological project of security. What is secured is not a nation but a sphere of influence that aims at becoming coextensive with the whole of human life. To use Solzhenitsyn's metaphor, the novel is an archipelago of knowledges that functions very much like a widely dispersed prison system. In *Gravity's Rainbow* Pynchon calls this region of actual and potential knowledges the 'Zone,' or an allocated area of epistemological experimentation where different orders of approximate knowledge are permitted to expand in all different directions while remaining theoretically accessible to some form of central military control.

The ordering frame within which Pynchon places the administration of all this minor knowledge is the museum. The most prominent archival facility in the novel, the 'White Visitation,' contains the slums of knowledge. The Palladian mansion housing this military intelligence complex has been 'preserved weatherless in some skin of clear museum plastic, an old-fashioned apparatus whose use has been forgotten.'[34] It contains 'a disused hospital for the mad, a few

token lunatics, an enormous pack of stolen dogs, cliques of spiritual-
ists, vaudeville entertainers, wireless technicians, Coueists, Ous-
penskians, Skinnerites, Dale Carnegie zealots, all exiled by the
outbreak of war from pet schemes and manias damned, had the
peace prolonged itself, to differing degrees of failure' (77). Pynchon's museum is a horizontal rather than a vertical space of
knowledges; it includes everything that state science has expelled to
margins and relegated to minorities. Throughout the novel it is never
entirely clear whether anything will come of all this research, but it
goes on anyway. There is no guarantee that the largely numerical
powers that the White Visitation directs at these different phenomena, calculation techniques which traverse the border between
mathematical science and social technology, will be even remotely
commensurate with what they seek to comprehend. The power of
the number has always played a decisive role in state operations such
as census, taxation and election. The numbers show that the patterning of Lt Slothrop's sexual conquests replicate the poisson distribution of V-2s falling over London. What the numbers cannot give is
anything like a complete representation of the objects they are
supposed to describe. At the end of the nineteenth century Kelvin
believed that '[w]hen you can measure what you are speaking about
and express it in numbers you know something about it; but when
you cannot measure it, when you cannot express it in numbers, your
knowledge is of a meagre and unsatisfactory kind.'[35] Much of the
novel's contradictory comic force turns on the question of whether
the military actually controls all the knowledge it is capable of
measuring. The White Visitation finally tries to come to terms with
Slothrop's psychokinetic powers by ordering this 'statistical oddity'
(85) castrated. More than once Pynchon intimates that, whoever
'They' are, they are the owners of a web of knowledge which they
have not mastered. 'Alas, the state of the art by 1945 was nowhere
near adequate to that kind of [perfect] data retrieval' (582).

  The frame of the Victorian museum may persist at the White
Visitation, but its contents display an irreversible tendency toward
entropy. Though it acts as a repository for various forms of essentia-
list thought, the White Visitation can never attain an essential
knowledge of the world. The museum on board the *Nautilus*
displayed knowledge as an eternally present spectacle with transparent origins and anthropocentric ends. By placing the nerve center of

Victorian epistemology in the hull of an advanced weapon, Verne accurately projected the development of the museum into a para-military state bureaucracy, what in 1948 Norbert Wiener would call an 'interscientific institute,' but what he did not foresee was that the continuing rationalization of the museum would by no means fulfill the central project of the imperial archive, namely, the construction of a positive and comprehensive knowledge of the world.[36] The White Visitation is a dissonant space of domination in which different orders of subjugated knowledge interact without coincid-ing. The facility does not dictate policy. It 'remains a colony to the metropolitan war' (76). Nothing there fits into an epistemological master pattern. The purpose of bringing together these outlying regions of knowledge baffles even the facility's commander, Briga-dier General Ernest Pudding, a classic Victorian archivist who has outlived his usefulness. The search for comprehensive knowledge has become outdated, so much so that Pudding has made a hobby of it, writing 'a mammoth work' (77), an unfinished-key-to-all-mytho-logies called *Things That Can Happen in European Politics*. The White Visitation is the wartime prototype of the modern museum that no longer produces the fiction that the knowledge it contains somehow constitutes a coherent representational universe, but under Pudding's command it nevertheless retains trace elements of an earlier order of things. Trained Baden-Powell style in military geography, Pudding, like Kipling's Colonel Creighton, 'was brought up to believe in a literal Chain of Command, as clergymen of earlier centuries believed in the Chain of Being. The newer geometries confuse him' (77).

'The newer geometries,' one of Pynchon's terms for the new magic epistemology, confuse General Pudding because he equates entropy with disorder, disorganization, disintegration. Though Pynchon repeatedly undercuts the totalizing project of the Victorian museum, he repeatedly intimates the existence of a new order of domination that works by keeping knowledges off-center. Perhaps the most famous premiss of *Gravity's Rainbow* is that it is actually possible to harness the disintegrating epistemologies of modern life. The novel takes a series of readings among various systems of knowledge to find that entropy does not in fact threaten or even destabilize existing orders of domination. Pynchon's cartels believe that entropy is good for business, forcing a mitosis of markets. The archivists in the White Visitation direct their gaze at knowledges which offer, at best, diminishing returns. The Zone itself is a utopia of entropies: a highly ordered space of disintegration populated by specialists who seek out the regularities of disintegration, the shape of the laws governing chance. Here it is worth remembering that disorder has its regularities; that if the organization of closed systems can only decrease irreversibly, the organization of open systems can succeed in managing entropy more or less indefinitely. For, according to Kelvin, entropy is systemic. This does not mean that things accumulate endlessly in an amorphous mass, or disappear at the mercy of chance events; rather it means that the forces of irregularity fall out in distinct patterns that serve to expand rather than contract the field of potential knowledges. The new magic epistemology is precisely an epistemology of expanding entropic knowledges, a coming-to-terms with the fact that all knowledge proliferates even as it entropies, and a massive institutional adjustment of the means of control to the entropic tendencies of information systems. It shades into mysticism precisely because it involves the statistical use of all available knowledges from the archive, whether dominant or subjugated, to predict the future.[37]

The entropic geometries which confuse Pudding came to be grouped under the rubric of cybernetics. Cybernetics was invented by a group of former military statisticians to come to terms with the tendency of information systems to fail. The difference between Pudding, a quintessential Victorian archivist, and most of the scientific personnel who populate Pynchon's novel is that the latter are perfectly aware of the failure of information systems to form a unified field. They maintain an immense resilience in the face of it, and over the course of the novel they produce an endless stream of discourse theorizing the problem of epistemological entropy. It appears as Murphy's Law, Gödel's Theorem, Maxwell's demon, Heisenberg's Uncertainty Principle, the problem of optimum prediction, the problem of axiomatic consistency. Whatever the name, the principle posits that the rules of any given system cannot encompass all contingency, and will ultimately be faced with exceptions that exist outside the structure of codification. In one sense, then, the new magic epistemology (cybernetics was its demobilized civilian name) was a way of coming to terms with exceptions to rules. It was less a form of control than a disposition to control; it posits the problem of control through indirection, and explores the possibility that incomplete or partial control may actually be preferable to full or complete control. The Allied high command maintains the White Visitation as a standing reserve of unrealized knowledges on the statistical off chance that some of them will amount to something. The White Visitation is Pynchon's favorite kind of social space: a potential assembling zone in which an arterial network of control systems intersect. The control achieved may be illusory – throughout the novel Pynchon maintains a second sense of control as a personality said to direct the statements of a spiritualist medium – or it may be very real. For the fact is that when the spirits appear at state-run seances, even they speak the twentieth century's dominant language of knowledge, the language of statistics (as when the ghost of Walter Rathenau, architect of the cartelized state, puts in an appearance to discourse on the nature of control).

The entropic epistemology of the White Visitation, with its universe governed by the laws of chance and statistics, goes a long way toward explaining new mutations of the invasion narrative visible throughout *Gravity's Rainbow*. In Pynchon's novel invasions do not take place on the surface of history. Nineteenth-century novels tended to represent test-tube invasions in which the mass and weight of armies were measured against the potential resistance offered by an indigenous population and its armed forces. Invasions took place in specialized fields (the English Channel, Alsace-Lorraine), under established circumstances (an overt declaration of war followed by a mass attack), and between clearly differentiated enemies (blues and reds and grays). These invasions all conformed to the regularities of Victorian thermodynamics in that they represented an entropic breaking down and breaking apart of complex organizations, generally armies faced with the friction of resistance (the standard for this narrative is undoubtedly the retreat in *War and Peace*). By contrast, the succession of invasions in *Gravity's Rainbow* represent a progressive reduction of thermodynamics to statistical mechanics: what the inventor of cybernetics, Norbert Wiener, called 'a reduction of the phenomena concerning heat and temperature to phenomena in which a Newtonian mechanics is applied to a situation in which we deal not with a single dynamical system but with a statistical distribution of dynamical systems; and in which our conclusions concern not all such systems but an overwhelming majority of them.'[38]

Gravity's Rainbow takes a spinning inventory of the invasion as a statistical and almost subterranean phenomenon. Though Pynchon does not aim at compiling a complete collection of data, he turns his attention to the long-term political mobility of entire populations, to vast movements of accumulation and slow saturation. His narrative does not contain a thick layer of dramatic historic events (D-Day appears only as the grain of Ike's voice on the radio). Rather Pynchon constructs an archeology of the various sedimentary strata of invasion that take place beneath the rapidly changing history of governments, wars, and famines. While the invasion novelists avoided tricky historical situations – hands off what occurred when the Oregon territory was being invaded simultaneously by the United States settlers, the British, the Mexicans, and the Russians – Pynchon represents invasion as an inextricable tangle of exploration, war, nomenclature, and laws. He seeks out precisely those situations in which invasion issues in neither colonization nor occupation but in a middle state of partial, incomplete, or pending colonization. *Gravity's Rainbow* abounds in accounts of the quintessential twentieth-century invasion, which involves the instrumentality not only of terrains but also of Herero birth rates, Cyrillic and Kirghiz alphabets, the nature of gravity. Far from being confined to a single geographical rubric, the invasion has become an exercise in manipulating lines of alliance (as Americans virtually occupy wartime London), enforcing new forms of suzerainty (as the Soviets impose their alphabet on Kirghizistan), and maintaining overlapping spheres of influence (in the Zone).[39] The statistical dynamics of the invasion cannot be separated from the study of geography and its long-term changes (Pynchon repeatedly refers to Alfred Wegener's classic 1915 work on continental drift), but neither can they be separated from the fabrication of models for economic growth, from the quantitative analysis of market movements, from accounts of demographic expansion and contraction, from the fixing of sociological constants, and from the modification of technological forms. The great subterranean invasions of the nineteenth century had been civilian mass migrations. In the twentieth century, Pynchon recognizes that invasion has become a form of military mass migration as, thanks to statistical mechanics, geography developed into demography, thus incorporating the complete existence of populations into the orbit of military planning.

The appearance of the long-duration invasion in the twentieth century, a form of invasiveness well suited to the features of statistical mechanics, applies equally well to the central invasion narrative of *Gravity's Rainbow*: the invasion of privacy and, finally, of personality. While statistical mechanics generally avows an agnosticism of the individual instance, Pynchon builds his novel around the premiss that the study of linear successions, for so long the object of statistical research, has given way to discoveries in what can be called statistical depth. Statistical depth is a method for defining and measuring interiority by documenting and classifying individual response to a sequence of possible choices. The assumption is that the identity of the individual, or the sense that the individual has depth, grows out of a linear succession of choices the individual makes. These choices tend to be reduced to simple binary divisions based on what Yule and Kendall, prominent 1930s British statisticians, call 'the *presence* or *absence* of some attribute in a series of individuals or objects' (11). At the White Visitation, Pointsman the statistician, 'like his master I. P. Pavlov before him . . . imagines the cortex of the brain as a mosaic of tiny on/off elements' (55). Slothrop's erections fascinate statisticians like Pointsman because they can only possess two values, limp and erect, off and on, zero and one. This attribute Slothrop shares with half the human race; the reason he takes on statistical depth is that his erections in response to German V-2s fall outside of the error function of the normal curve of probability. For statisticians, Slothrop takes on depth precisely because his response has become progressively differentiated from the corporate norm. His individuality is strictly the result of statistical anomaly, and as such it provokes various forms of documentary invasion aimed at reckoning with the exception that proves the rule – the exception that confirms the rule by testing it at its outer reaches.

The model of statistical depth, however, does not entail 'the stone determinacy of everything' (86), for the simple reason that the forms of documentation out of which it constructs personality are often incompatible. Over the course of the novel Pynchon develops a mass of documentation with which the identity of Tyrone Slothrop is inextricably linked. In no way can the identity of Slothrop be

separated from the material documentation (texts, accounts, registers, transcripts, laws, techniques, customs) expended on him in
succession by various documentary authorities. The form of his
individuality cannot be separated, in other words, from the consciously organized forms of documentation that exist around and
even through him, at every time and in every place. Sometimes we
eavesdrop on Slothrop's adventures through the medium of sodium-
amytal-induced interrogation; at other times his personality takes
shape in and through a sequence of personality tests, Rohrschach
blots, Bernreuter Inventories, Minnesota Multiphasic Personality
Tests. Nevertheless all this statistical documentation of personality
never assumes the status of definitively acquired knowledge. Pynchon issues Slothrop not one but many identity cards; as the novel
progresses it becomes clear that Slothrop's papers are in vast and
epic disorder. In a very real sense the technical play of bureaucratic
languages in *Gravity's Rainbow* must be understood as an effort to
follow the formation and transformations of a body of statistical
knowledge about a given subject. As a subject it seems to be
Slothrop's fate to be experimented on, conditioned and overcondi-
tioned, constituted over and over again.

The only architectonic unity which this mass of documentation
can possibly possess is imaginary, and in *Gravity's Rainbow* this
imagined unity of knowledges goes by the name of paranoia.
Paranoia reveals forms of connection, preserves hierarchies of
importance, reveals networks of determination. Paranoia is a fear of
the archive, a fear that the fundamental codes of a culture's archive –
those governing its languages, its schemas of perception, its
exchanges, its geographies – have been deciphered. Behind all visible
events and invisible correspondences it perceives and positions a
force so powerful, and a power so forceful, that it underlies even the
simplest forms of order. The imperial archive had imagined that all
forms of order were finally subject to state control; even the ordering
capabilities of enemy archives were represented as being answerable
to states such as Germany. Paranoia perceives that the ordering
agencies of modern life are no longer national in character or scope
such that they can fall into the hands of discrete enemies. In
Gravity's Rainbow the basic agent of state control has become the
archive itself. This is no mere Wizard of Oz control fantasy. More
than anything else, Slothrop fears that a new kind of counter-

rational rationality now orders knowledge. He fears, in other words, that what has been called the new magic epistemology has become anterior to perceptions, gestures, words. Even in the inflection of the voices of his lovers, Katje Borgesius and Geli Tripping, he hears the voice of an authority which, he imagines, has succeeded in orchestrating the basic ordering codes of life.

The search for the basic ordering code of life was the very lifeblood of the imperial archive. Cracking that code was both the basis of the nineteenth century's dreams of knowledge, and the basis of its nightmares. The British Museum established a network of lifelines for feeding that knowledge to the state, which increasingly devoted itself less to interpreting knowledge than to storing it. Outside of the state, anyone who came close to unraveling the knot of comprehensive knowledge was by definition an enemy. Victorian Fausts invariably found themselves tempted into a hell of order, and in Victorian literature the ordering impulse is always closely allied with exile, ostracism, madness. Outside of the state, the archive is hell, and Victorian archivists are the lineal descendants of the damned. Even in the late twentieth century Pynchon can still figure hell as a 'very extensive museum, a place of many levels, and new wings that generate like living tissue – though if it all does grow toward some end shape, those who are here inside can't see it' (537). The image is striking: a museum that develops into higher states of disorganization even as it expands. The figuration of an enemy archive was yet another way of trying to get outside the expanding entropic universe of a culture's archive, projecting its double so as to attempt to see it in its totality. An enemy stands far enough outside a culture to see its basic outlines; an enemy is an Archimedean point through which a culture articulates its unspoken structures of perception and thought. In this sense an enemy archive was and is an imaginary parallel universe through which a culture articulates its archive as a totality by producing representations of alien ideologies (as irrevocably Other), nationalities (as space-invaders), and phenomena (as Unidentified Flying Objects). The idea of the enemy archive is one of the last remnants of the imperial archive, and it forms the basis for the most modern of narratives, science fiction.

In *The Order of Things* Foucault maintains that cultures cannot with complete certainty plumb the unspoken orders which form the mythology of their knowledges. In *Gravity's Rainbow*, however, the order of things has become something that can be accessed. 'They know in London how to draw pentacles too, and cry conjurations, how to bring in exactly the ones they want.' Now not only dominant but also subjugated knowledges have been laid open to the probes of an enemy without shape, definition, name, or substance. This enemy, this 'They,' is the modern state. In the nineteenth century people like Verne and Childers foresaw the degree to which the state would become dependent on subjugated and local knowledges. But Verne comes close to equating the state with individual agency, Childers with national agency. In *20,000 Leagues* the visible world is subject to Nemo's individual agency; in *The Riddle of the Sands*, even the most derealized of perceptual fields is subject to the national agency of German planning. In *Gravity's Rainbow* the modern state is neither a race of archival supermen nor a national supergovernment. In Pynchon's novel all the world's states resonate together, raise armies for themselves that act less in conflict than in concert (in the Zone the military acts primarily as a police force), and exhibit a unity of composition in spite of their differences in organization and development.[40] The state now extends into the 'Other Side,' Pynchon's wonderful term that collapses the extraterrestrial (the beyond) with the extraterritorial (the enemy). In the twentieth century the state has become a magical operation, full of what Marx once called 'a cosmopolitan, universal energy which overflows every restriction and bond so as to establish itself instead as the sole bond.'[41] The sense of quantitative agency upon which the imperial archive predicated its construction of knowledges has been destroyed. What is left is a qualitative agency superintended by a new magic epistemology that effectively reverses Comte's chain of historical development. Comte said that religious knowledge would in time give way to positive knowledge. In Pychon's novel positive knowledge recedes back into myth and religion. The superintending states no longer care what orders of knowledge they are collecting. They no longer even care what knowledge is, so long as they have it. The state is neutral about knowledge so long as knowledge belongs to the state. At the end of Pynchon's novel the White Visitation shuts its doors. The museum is no longer the privileged archive of culture; the archive, the sum total of what can or cannot be said or done, has become the very form of the modern state.

NOTES

CHAPTER ONE

1. Michel Foucault, *The Archaeology of Knowledge* (New York 1972), p. 130; Arthur Conan Doyle, 'The Empty House,' in *The Return of Sherlock Holmes* (Harmondsworth 1981), p. 17.
2. 'Tibet is a special case. Tibet was deliberately set aside by the Empire *as* free and neutral territory, a Switzerland for the spirit where there is no extradition, an Alp-Himalayas to draw the soul upward, and danger rare enough to tolerate'; Thomas Pynchon, *Gravity's Rainbow* (New York 1987), p. 321. For a systematic overview of the formation of the image of Tibet within imperial mythology, see Peter Bishop, *The Myth of Shangri-La: Tibet, Travel Writing and the Western Creation of Sacred Landscape* (Berkeley 1989). For Madam Blavatsky on Tibet, see *The Book of Golden Precepts* (London 1889); *The Voice of the Silence* (London 1889).
3. The classic anatomy of the breakdown of 'a universalistic way of thinking' in late nineteenth-century thought is Ernst Cassirer, *The Problem of Knowledge: Philosophy, Science, and History Since Hegel* (New Haven 1950). For Cassirer on Kant's program for universal knowledge, see pp. 14ff.
4. 'Surveying,' *Encyclopaedia Britannica*, 11th edition, vol. 26 (London 1911), p. 151; Edwin Abbott, *Flatland: A Romance of Many Dimensions* (New York 1963), p. 48.
5. Despite various attempts to invent a long tradition for the Secret Service (as in Richard Deacon's *A History of the British Secret Service* [London 1969]), spying was a rudimentary and informal business in the nineteenth century. In India as elsewhere, it tended to result from close personal and intellectual ties among individuals belonging to elite institutions such as clubs, universities, and learned societies. For an

examination of the way in which, in nineteenth-century Britain, 'control of official information was exercised though an informal code of conduct among the elite group of politicians and administrators, who had a strong common interest in treating the conduct of public affairs as an essentially private matter,' see Clive Ponting, *Secrecy in Britain* (Oxford 1990).

6. A number of works deal with the imagined universality of the British Museum in the nineteenth century. Richard Garnett saw quite clearly that his archive had undertaken 'an utopian project'; see 'The British Museum Catalogue as the Basis of a Universal Catalogue,' *Essays in Librarianship and Bibliography* (London 1899), pp. 109–14. Edward Miller emphasizes the international diversification of the institution in *That Noble Cabinet: A History of the British Museum* (Athens, Ohio 1974). For an institutional history of Catalogue debates (one that does not begin to do justice to the museum's status as myth), see Barbara McCrimmon, *Power, Politics, and Print: The Publication of the British Museum Catalogue, 1881–1900* (Hamden, Conn. 1981). For a sense of the museum explicitly as myth in nineteenth-century French literature, see Eugenio Donato, 'The Museum's Furnace: Notes Toward a Contextual Reading of *Bouvard and Pecuchet*,' in Josué V. Harari, ed., *Textual Strategies: Perspectives in Post-Structuralist Criticism* (Ithaca, N.Y. 1979), pp. 213–38. Michel Serres also underscores the mythical character of Victorian epistemologies in *Hermes: Literature, Science, Philosophy* (Baltimore 1982).

7. 'Without detailed records, centralized administration is almost inconceivable, and numerical tabulation has long been recognized as an especially convenient form for certain kinds of information'; Theodore M. Porter, *The Rise of Statistical Thinking, 1820–1900* (Princeton, N.J. 1986), p. 17.

8. Benedict Anderson stresses the 'modular' character of the colonial administrative apparatuses, 'capable of being transplanted, with varying degrees of self-consciousness, to a great variety of social terrains, to merge and be merged with a correspondingly wide variety of political and ideological constellations'; *Imagined Communities: Reflections on the Origin and Spread of Nationalism* (London 1983), p. 14.

9. The interminable reports on the condition and constitution of the British Museum that Parliament generated every ten years or so throughout the nineteenth century provide the best introduction to this decentralization of knowledge within the museum. The most lively of these texts is the 1850 *Report of the Commissioners Appointed to Inquire into the Constitution and Government of the British Museum*, which includes some craggy testimony from Thomas Carlyle. The

standard text on the fragmentation of the 'grand narratives' of the nineteenth century is Jean-François Lyotard, *The Postmodern Condition: A Report on Knowledge* (Minneapolis 1984). On T.E. Lawrence's involvement with British Museum expeditions, see B.H. Liddell Hart, *Lawrence of Arabia* (1935; New York 1989), pp. 3–20.

10. Carl von Clausewitz, *On War* (Princeton, N.J. 1976), p. 214.

11. T.G. Montgomerie, 'On the Geographical Position of Yarkund, and Some Other Places in Central Asia,' *Journal of the Royal Geographical Society* 36 (1866), p. 157. Other particulars of the expedition appear in Survey of India Department, *Exploration in Tibet and Neighbouring Regions*, Part 1, *1865–1879*, Part 2, *1879–1892* (Dehra Dun, India 1915). Of the various memoirs dealing with the exploration of Tibet, the best was written by one of the pundits, Sarat Chandra Das, the model for Kipling's Hurree Babu; *Journey to Lhasa and Central Tibet* (London 1902).

12. The OED lists the first senses of *reading* as 'readout' occurring in 1833, 1838, and 1869.

13. Montgomerie, 'On the Geographical Position,' p. 167.

14. Rudyard Kipling, *Kim* (Harmondsworth 1987), p. 59. Further citations appear in the text.

15. Franz Kafka, *The Complete Stories* (New York 1971), pp. 235, 416. Gilles Deleuze and Felix Guattari quote a key passage from 'An Old Manuscript' near the beginning of '1227: Treatise on Nomadology – The War Machine,' in *A Thousand Plateaus: Capitalism and Schizophrenia* (Minneapolis 1987), p. 353.

16. Colonel Thomas H. Holdich, *Tibet the Mysterious* (New York 1906), p. 233.

17. Samuel Butler, *Erewhon* (Harmondsworth 1970), p. 167. Sven Hedin's account of the procedure by which he took 'nine photographs, forming a consecutive series' appears in *Trans-Himalaya: Discoveries and Adventures in Tibet*, Volume 2 (London 1909), pp. 102–3.

18. This passage from Royce forms the basis for Jorge Luis Borges's fantasy of a perfect cartographical simulacrum in 'Partial Enchantments of the Quixote,' in *Other Inquisitions, 1937–1952* (Austin, Texas 1964), pp. 43–6. See Josiah Royce, *The World and the Individual* (New York 1900).

19. This deterritorialized occupation is the precursor of the Palestinian withdrawal from Palestine, a diaspora that Paul Virilio has called 'the end of on the spot civil defense, since the mechanical power of the new armies of the State have forced the . . . combatant to withdraw provisionally from the soil he is supposed to protect'; 'Popular Defense

and Popular Assault,' in *Autonomia: Post-Political Politics, Semio-text(e)* III, 3 (1980), p. 268.

20. 'The State needs to subordinate hydraulic force to conduits, pipes, embankments, which prevent turbulence, which constrain movement to go from one point to another, and space itself to be striated and measured, which makes the fluid depend on the solid, and flows proceed by parallel, laminar layers'; Deleuze and Guattari, 'Treatise on Nomadology,' p. 363. Here it is worth recalling that in 1853 the British conceived of the Indian railway system explicitly with a view to administrative and military control.

21. In his cyberpunk novel *Neuromancer*, William Gibson describes a computer virus that works in a Kim-like way: 'This ain't bore and inject, it's more like we interface with the ice [an information block] so slow, the ice doesn't feel it. The face of the Kuang logics kinda sleazes up to the target and mutates, so it gets to be exactly like the ice fabric. Then we lock on and the main programs cut in, start talkin' circles' round the logics on the ice. We go Siamese twin on 'em before they even get restless' (New York 1984), p. 169.

22. Pierre Clastres, *Society Against the State* (New York 1987), p. 218.

23. Ludwig Boltzmann, 'Über die Grundprinzipien und Grundgleichungen der Mechanik,' quoted in Porter, *Rise of Statistical Thinking*, p. 208.

24. The 'Go' model is another way of talking about Foucault's sense of the 'play of . . . location, arrangement, and replacement' that characterizes systems of 'dispersed and heterogeneous' statements; see *The Archaeology of Knowledge*, p. 34. Attempts to maintain the chess analogy in modern strategic discourse generally degenerate into a tangle of modifications; witness B.H. Liddell Hart in his classic *Strategy* (1964):

> While air-mobility could achieve such direct strokes by an overhead form of indirect approach, tank-mobility might achieve them by an indirect approach on the ground avoiding the 'obstacle' of the opposing army. To illustrate the point by a board-game analogy, with chess – air-mobility introduced a knight's move, and tank-mobility a queen's move, into warfare. This analogy does not, of course, express their respective values. For an air-force combined the vaulting power of the knight's move with the all-ways flexibility of the queen's move. On the other hand, a mechanized ground force, though it lacked vaulting power, could remain in occupation of the 'square' it gained.

> Recall, too, that in his *Dictionary of Received Ideas* Flaubert defined chess as 'symbol of military tactics.'

25. Friedrich Nietzsche, *The Gay Science* (New York 1974).

26. See Arthur Conolly, 'Overland Invasion of India,' in *Journey to the North of India*, Volume 2 (London 1838), pp. 321–58.
27. Deleuze and Guattari, 'Treatise on Nomadology,' p. 353.
28. On 'Russification,' see Anderson, *Imagined Communities*, pp. 104–6. Here it is worth recalling that Lyotard's sense of the break-up of grand narratives into practical narratives and finally into narratives of autonomy almost exactly recapitulates the trajectory of decolonization. So closely does the Lahore Museum approximate local interests that in time it becomes indistinguishable from them.
29. Paul Virilio, *Speed and Politics: An Essay on Dromology* (New York 1986), p. 94.
30. In his introduction to the Penguin edition of *Kim*, Edward Said justly calls attention to the central position Creighton occupies in the novel.
31. The one exception is when the most peace-loving person in the novel, the Lama, gets cudgeled by the Russians. Given the fates of Mahatma Gandhi, Martin Luther King, and Anwar Sadat, this nonviolent provocation of violence is hardly exceptional. In the novel, however, it has a contradictory comic force, a little bit like the Mel Brooks silent movie in which Marcel Marceau is the only one who speaks. Virilio advances his theory of peacetime war in *Speed and Politics*, p. 142.
32. The domino theory of its day, this remarkable calculation appears to have been no big secret; Thomas Holdich discusses it at some length in the 'Tibet' article he wrote for the 11th edition of the *Encyclopaedia Britannica* in 1911.
33. L. Austine Waddell, *Lhasa and Its Mysteries, With a Record of the British Tibetan Expedition of 1903–1904* (New York 1988), p. 58.
34. J.G. Ballard's novel *Empire of the Sun* (1960) opens in the British zone of Shanghai, which the Japanese invaded and occupied in 1941. On the Japanese attack, see A. Morgan Young, *Imperial Japan 1926–1938* (London 1938); Christopher Thorne, *The Limits of Foreign Policy: The West, the League, and the Far Eastern Crisis of 1931–1933* (London 1972); James William Morley, ed., *Japan Erupts: The London Naval Conference and the Manchurian Incident 1928–1932* (New York 1984).
35. Erich Ludendorff, *The Nation at War* (London 1936), pp. 14, 15–16. Most historians now regard the American Civil War as the first total war, but the idea of complete war did not achieve currency until the early 1930s.
36. 'If air, water, the elasticity of steam, and the pressure of the atmosphere, were of different qualities; if they could be appropriated, and each quality existed only in moderate abundance, they, as well as the land, would afford a rent, as the successive qualities were brought into use';

David Ricardo, *On the Principles of Political Economy*, quoted in Deleuze and Guattari, 'Treatise on Nomadology,' p. 567.

37. James Hilton, *Lost Horizon* (New York 1939), p. 22. Further citations appear in the text.

38. J.D. Salinger wonderfully summons up this aerial interconnection between cities and states when he has a character tell a spy story about crossing 'the Paris–Chinese border'; see 'The Laughing Man,' in *Nine Stories* (New York 1964), pp. 56–73. Nineteenth- and early-twentieth-century visions of air travel almost always project air travel as privatized and individual rather than collective and state supervised; see, for example, Isaac Asimov, ed., *Futuredays: A Nineteenth-Century Vision of the Year 2000* (London 1986). The modern system of air regulations was already in place by the time J. Parker Van Zandt wrote *The Geography of World Air Transport* (Washington D.C. 1944).

39. See Georges Bataille, 'The Unarmed Society: Lamaism,' in *The Accursed Share: An Essay on General Economy*, Volume 1, *Consumption* (New York 1988), pp. 93–110.

40. For an overview of the history of the fortress, see Henry Guerlac, 'Vauban: The Impact of Science on War,' in Peter Paret, ed., *Makers of Modern Strategy: Military Thought from Machiavelli to Hitler* (Princeton, N.J. 1986), pp. 64–90.

41. Lewis Mumford, *Technics and Civilization* (New York 1963), p. 11.

42. In the book Conway leaves at Mallinson's behest; to supply suitable motivation the movie goes so far as to transform Mallinson from a subaltern into Conway's brother, 'George.'

A variant on Cold War ideology, sentimental survivalism has not received the critical attention it deserves. The quintessential example comes in the film *Failsafe* (1964), when the President of the United States orders the destruction of New York City. The film makes it clear that he unleashes a nuclear holocaust in the name of humanity. The refrain to 'We'll Meet Again' accompanying the nuclear blasts at the end of *Dr Strangelove* (1963) highlights the same phenomenon.

43. Thomas Malthus, *A Summary View of the Principle of Population* (1830; Harmondsworth 1982), p. 223.

44. In the same way, David Brower, archdruid of the environmental movement in the 1970s and 1980s and opponent of new technologies of movement, naturalizes the railroad technology of his youth. John McPhee sums up this logic: 'A railroad over the Sierra is all right. It was there. An interstate highway is an assault on the terrain'; see *Encounters with an Archdruid* (New York 1971), p. 29.

45. This is precisely the problem of the 'mine-shaft gap' in Kubrick's *Dr*

Strangelove: which state will be the first to reconsolidate its control in a post-apocalyptic world?

46. The High Lama's view of states as interfering with the circulation of information has a premonitory force. As Lyotard later recognized, 'the notion that learning falls within the purview of the State, as the brain or mind of society, will become more and more outdated with the increasing strength of the opposing principle, according to which society exists and progresses only if the messages circulating within it are rich in information and easy to decode'; *Postmodern Condition*, p. 5.

47. On the nineteenth-century invention of global ideology, see Dietmar Kamper and Cristoph Wulf, eds., *Looking Back on the End of the World* (New York 1989). Oswald Spengler explicitly situates the decline of the West within the breakdown and entropy of imperial epistemological channels; see 'The State,' in *The Decline of the West*, Volume 2 (New York 1980), pp. 327–435.

48. Karl Mannheim, *Ideology and Utopia: An Introduction to the Sociology of Knowledge* (New York 1936), pp. 160–61. My account of Mannheim's position draws on Martin Jay, *Marxism and Totality* (Berkeley 1984), p. 207.

49. Jürgen Habermas constructs a genealogy of the ideology of communicative transparency within the British public sphere in *The Structural Transformation of the Public Sphere* (1962; Cambridge 1989). In this work Habermas vacillates uneasily between viewing the public sphere as an institution and as an ideological construction; in later work he tends to elevate it from the status of hypostatis to the status of fact. It ought to be clear that I regard the 'public sphere' as belonging to the mythic domain of ideology.

50. For a critique of information as pure instrumentality, see William Leiss, 'The Myth of the Information Society,' in Ian Angus and Sut Jhally, eds., *Cultural Politics in Contemporary America* (New York 1989).

CHAPTER TWO

1. Darwin once said of morphology, 'This is the most interesting department of natural history, and may be said to be its very soul' (quoted in George Gaylord Simpson, 'Anatomy and Morphology: Classification and Evolution: 1859 and 1959,' in *Proceedings of the American Philosophical Society*, vol. 103, no. 23, April 1959, p. 289).

Basic introductions to the position of morphology in nineteenth-century biology can be found in William Coleman, *Biology in the*

Nineteenth Century: Problems of Form, Function, and Transformation (Cambridge 1977); Ernst Mayr, *The Growth of Biological Thought: Diversity, Evolution, and Inheritance* (Cambridge 1982); and Ernst Cassirer, 'The Ideal of Knowledge and its Transformation in Biology,' in *The Problem of Knowledge* (New Haven 1950). The reaction against morphology in twentieth-century biology receives attention in Garland Allen, *Life Science in the Twentieth Century* (Cambridge 1978). The classic text announcing 'the cleavage between morphology and biophysics or biochemistry' is Joseph Needham, *Order and Life* (Cambridge 1936).

2. See Auguste Comte, 'General View of Biology' (from *Cours de Philosophie Positive* [1838–1842]), in *Auguste Comte and Positivism: The Essential Writings* (Chicago 1983), pp. 163–81.

3. Linnaeus, *Philosophie botanique*, Section 299, quoted in Michel Foucault, 'Classifying,' in *The Order of Things: An Archaeology of the Human Sciences* (New York 1973), p. 134.

4. Charles Darwin, *The Voyage of the Beagle* (New York 1988), p. 17.

5. The later Darwin preserves this taxonomic optimism: 'We could not . . . define the several groups; but we could pick out types, or forms, representing the characters of each group, whether large or small, and thus give a general idea of the value of the differences between them. This is what we should be driven to if we were ever to succeed in collecting all the forms in any class which have lived throughout all time and space. We shall certainly never succeed in making so perfect a collection: nevertheless, in certain classes, we are tending in this direction . . . ' (quoted in George Gaylord Simpson, 'Anatomy and Morphology,' p. 299).

6. Charles Darwin, 'Mutual Affinities of Organic Beings: Morphology: Embryology: Rudimentary Organs,' in *The Origin of Species* (Harmondsworth 1968; orig. pub. 1859), pp. 397–434.

7. Michel Foucault says that 'the monster ensures the *emergence* of difference' (my emphasis), but I believe that this formulation must be altered. What ensures the emergence of difference is the expansion of Europe into the colonial world. The position of the monster within the Linnaean scheme allows only for the placement of difference in a taxonomy, where its emergence is effectively confined and prevented from becoming a very threatening event. See 'Classifying,' in *The Order of Things*, pp. 155–7.

8. See Kurt Gödel, 'On Formally Undecidable Propositions in [Alfred North Whitehead's] *Principia Mathematica* [1911]' (1931).

9. This sequence of logical reversals in Alice's adventures follows the analysis of Gilles Deleuze in *The Logic of Sense* (New York 1990), pp.

2–3. Because most of the quotations from the Alice texts are quite familiar, I have dispensed with page citations.

10. D'Arcy Thompson, *On Growth and Form* (Cambridge 1961); orig. pub. 1917), p. 293.

11. Ibid., pp. 274–5.

12. The idea of the 'mutant' at first encompassed primarily the possibility of discontinuous variation. The possibility of artificial cloning began with the 1891 experiments of Hans Driesch, which showed that organisms may develop not only out of eggs but also out of certain cells caught at an early embryonic phase. The science of H.G. Wells's *The Island of Dr. Moreau* (1896) strikes an uneasy balance between Driesch's findings and the emphasis within late-Victorian morphology on discontinuous variation. One of the earliest texts on the viability of cloning is Jacques Loeb, *The Organism as a Whole from a Physio-chemical Viewpoint* (1916).

13. Bram Stoker, *Dracula* (Oxford 1983; orig. pub. 1897), p. 10. Subsequent citations appear in the text.

14. Charles Darwin, *The Formation of Vegetable Mould through the Action of Worms* (Ontario, California 1976), p. 145. Stoker was obsessed by the functions of worms and returned to them in his 1911 novel, *The Lair of the White Worm*.

15. Fanon quite frequently uses the image of living death to describe the plight of colonial peoples. 'The culture once living and open to the future, becomes closed, fixed in the colonial status, caught in the yoke of oppression. Both present and mummified, it testifies against its members. . . . The cultural mummification leads to a mummification of individual thinking. . . . As though it were possible for a man to evolve otherwise than within the framework of a culture that recognizes him and that he decides to assume.' Frantz Fanon, 'Racism and Culture,' in *Toward an African Revolution* (London 1970), p. 44. Fanon's classic anatomy of the alienated colonial intellectual is *Black Skin White Masks* (London 1970).

16. See Alfred W. Crosby, *Ecological Imperialism: The Biological Expansion of Europe, 900–1900* (Cambridge 1986). Stoker's text has a prospective character for the twentieth century: it reverses the flow of disease to the colonial world and figures the biological *contraction* of Europe. On the problem of Dracula's coming to England, see Stephen Arata, 'The Occidental Tourist: Dracula and the Anxiety of Reverse Colonization,' *Victorian Studies*, vol. 33, no. 4 (1990), pp. 621–45.

17. These are of course the classic functions of absolutism as enumerated by Perry Anderson in *Lineages of the Absolutist State* (London 1974).

18. Any number of agreements, foremost among them the Berlin Congress

of 1878, contrived to keep the edge of Europe secure so that the great powers could concentrate on expansion in the colonial world. On the centrality of the Eastern Question in nineteenth-century politics, see Franz Ansprenger, *The Dissolution of the Colonial Empires* (London 1989); Richard Millman, *Britain and the Eastern Question, 1875–1878* (Oxford 1979); and G. D. Clayton, *Britain and the Eastern Question: Missolonghi to Gallipoli* (London 1971).

19. Joseph Needham, *Biochemistry and Morphogenesis* (Cambridge 1950; orig. pub. 1942), p. xv.

20. The concern with form has often led many to an obsession with formalism. On the use of morphological concepts as the basic vocabulary for a variety of aestheticisms, see G.S. Rousseau, ed., *Organic Form: The Life of an Idea* (London 1972), and Lancelot Law Whyte, ed., *Aspects of Form: Symposium on Nature and Art* (Bloomington 1951).

21. On the structure and behavior of crystals, see A. C. Bishop, *An Outline of Crystal Morphology* (London 1967) and Donald E. Sands, *Introduction to Crystallography* (New York 1969). For an examination of the role played by crystallography in the history of morphology, see John G. Burke, *Origins of the Science of Crystals* (Berkeley 1966).

22. 'By exceptional being, I mean not a monster or a natural marvel, but a rare statistical entity.' Simone de Beauvoir, *Force of Circumstance* (Harmondsworth 1968; orig. pub. 1963), p. 276. This is of course the status of Slothrop in Pynchon's *Gravity's Rainbow*, where, instead of monsters, there are prodigies of improbability. On the epistemology of probability, see Lorenz Kruger et al., eds., *The Probabilistic Revolution*, Volumes 1 and 2 (Cambridge, Mass. 1987).

23. Goethe, quoted in Philip C. Ritterbush, 'Organic Form: Aesthetics and Objectivity in the Study of Form in the Life Sciences,' in *Organic Form*, 35.

24. J.G. Ballard, *The Crystal World* (New York 1966), p. 77. Subsequent citations appear in the text.

25. On the nineteenth-century invention of the 'end of the world,' see Dietmar Kamper and Christoph Wulf, eds., *Looking Back on the End of the World* (New York 1989).

26. On the failure of all philosophers of totality, see Michel Serres, *Hermes: Literature, Science, Philosophy* (Baltimore 1982). René Thom offers one of the more recent attempts to update morphology by constructing paradigms for discontinuous change, in *Structural Stability and Morphogenesis* (Redwood City, California 1972). Today the general rubric for this new aestheticism of spiralling forms is 'chaotic dynamics,' which is basically an attempt to revive morphological explanation as a

paradigm for the physical sciences. Its unapologetic formalism has won wide appeal, and it may well find its final resting place not in thesciences but in the humanities, where it evidently serves as fuel for a new formalism. For evidence of this direction, see James Gleick, *Chaos* (New York 1987) and N. Katherine Hayles, *Chaos Bound: Orderly Disorder in Contemporary Literature and Science* (Ithaca 1990).

27. Joseph Needham, *Biochemistry and Morphogenesis*, p. xvi.

CHAPTER THREE

1. On the power of the imaginary ideological construction of the late Victorian nation-state, see Benedict Anderson, *Imagined Communities: Reflections on the Origin and Spread of Nationalism* (London 1983).
2. Thomas Hobbes, *Leviathan* (Harmondsworth 1985), p. 223.
3. On the formation and consolidation of the bourgeois public sphere, see Jürgen Habermas, *The Structural Transformation of the Public Sphere: An Inquiry into a Category of Bourgeois Society* (Cambridge, Mass. 1989), p. 27.
4. Alfred Thayer Mahan, 'Discussion of the Elements of Sea Power,' *The Influence of Sea Power Upon History, 1660–1783* (New York 1987), pp. 25–89.
5. On the status of positivist conceptions of knowledge within the British scientific community in the nineteenth century, see David Oldroyd, 'Nineteenth-Century Positivism,' *The Arch of Knowledge: An Introductory Study of the History and Philosophy and Methodology of Science* (New York 1986), pp. 168–208.
6. There is a vast secondary literature on the persistence of the mechanistic epistemology in classical mechanics, hydrodynamics, and thermodynamics. A good point of entry is R.C. Olby et al., eds., *Companion to the History of Modern Science* (London 1990). The classic text on the genealogy of mechanism as epistemology is E.J. Dijksterhuis, *The Mechanization of the World Picture: Pythagoras to Newton* (Princeton 1986). On mechanism and dynamics, see Richard S. Westfall, *The Construction of Modern Science: Mechanisms and Mechanics* (Cambridge 1977). Newton's own work still compels attention for its unrivalled elegance and clarity; see the two volumes of the *Principia*, *The Motion of Bodies* and *The System of the World* in Motte's translation (Berkeley 1934).
7. On Maxwell's development of unified field theory, see P. M. Harman, 'Matter and Force: Ether and Field Theories,' *Energy, Force and*

Matter: The Conceptual Development of Nineteenth-Century Physics (Cambridge 1982), pp. 72–119. This is the best recent book on the ways in which thermodynamics manifested a tacit dependence on the mechanistic epistemology; Harman usefully appends in his bibliographic essay the enormous primary and secondary literature on thermodynamics, pp. 156–76.

8. On the status of the mechanical model, see Harman, 'The Decline of the Mechanical World View,' Energy, Force, and Matter, pp. 149–55.

9. James Clerk Maxwell, Theory of Heat (New York 1872), p. 309. Subsequent citations appear in the text. On the development of probability to and after Maxwell, see the two volumes of The Probabilistic Revolution, Ideas in History and Ideas in the Sciences, edited by Lorenz Kruger et al. (Cambridge, Mass. 1987). On statistics generally, see Stephen M. Stigler, The History of Statistics: The Measurement of Uncertainty before 1900 (Cambridge, Mass. 1986).

10. See Henry Mayhew, London Labour and the London Poor, edited by Victor Neuburg (Harmondsworth 1985); William Farr, Eighth Annual Report of the Registrar-General of Births, Deaths, and Marriages, in England (London 1848). For a wide-ranging survey of the status of information within biological taxonomies, see Ernst Mayr, 'Microtaxonomy, The Science of Species,' The Growth of Biological Thought: Diversity, Evolution, Inheritance (Cambridge, Mass. 1982), pp. 251–297.

11. For a survey of the more extreme applications of the concept of entropy to ordered structures, especially within the rhetoric of social prophecy, see Greg Myers, 'Nineteenth-Century Popularizations of Thermodynamics and the Rhetoric of Social Prophecy,' in Patrick Brantlinger, ed., Energy and Entropy: Science and Culture in Victorian Britain (Bloomington 1989), pp. 307–38.

12. Herman Melville, Moby-Dick, quoted in James Gleick, Chaos: Making a New Science (New York 1987), p. 301.

13. James Clerk Maxwell, letter to Peter Guthrie Tait (1867), quoted in Harman, Energy, Force, and Matter, p. 139.

14. Jorge Luis Borges, 'Of Exactitude in Science,' in A Universal History of Infamy (Harmondsworth 1975), p. 131.

15. René Thom, Structural Stability and Morphogenesis (Redwood City 1972), pp. 9, 16, 47.

16. As Maxwell formulates it, the First Law of Thermodynamics (mandating the conservation of energy) states that 'when work is transformed into heat, or heat into work, the quantity of work is mechanically equivalent to the quantity of heat.' Theory of Heat, p. 152. On the position of Carnot's vessel in cultural history, see Michel Serres,

'Turner Translates Carnot,' in Josue V. Harari and David F. Bell, eds., *Hermes: Literature, Science, Philosophy* (Baltimore 1982), pp. 54–62.

17. Maxwell extends Carnot's sense of the limitations of his engine in *Theory of Heat*, p. 139ff.

18. Jules Verne, *Journey to the Centre of the Earth* (1864; Harmondsworth 1965). For a sense of the centrality of the discipline of meteorology in nineteenth-century thought, see Cleveland Abbe, 'Meteorology,' in *Encyclopaedia Britannica*, 11th edition (New York 1911), XVIII, pp. 264–91.

19. The German high command had been rightly skeptical about the use of such unpredictable weapons, but German policy was largely dictated by the chemical monopolies that had developed the technology in the first place. Victor Lefebure indicts 'the great German I.G., the Interessen Gemeinschaft, the world power in organic enterprise, whose monopoly existence threatened to turn the tide of war against us.' See *The Riddle of the Rhine: Chemical Strategy in Peace and War* (New York 1923), p. 18.

20. John Ruskin, 'The Storm-Cloud of the Nineteenth Century' (1884), in *The Norton Anthology of English Literature, Volume Two* (New York 1979), pp. 1341–2.

21. Ruskin offers a vivid picture of the entropic levelling of the hot and the cold: 'In those old days, when weather was fine, it was luxuriously fine; when it was bad – it was often abominably bad, but it had its fit of temper and was done with it – it didn't sulk for three months without letting you see the sun' (ibid., p. 1338).

22. Ibid., p. 1347.

23. To be precise, Arnold regards disorder as whatever social forces happen to be external to the cultured bourgeoisie; see *Culture and Anarchy* (New York 1941). See also J. A. Hobson's analysis of imperialism as a response to a capitalist economy of diminishing returns, in *Imperialism: A Study* (1902; Ann Arbor 1965). Hobson regards the military character of late Victorian imperialism as a measure of the desperation brought on by tightening economic conditions.

24. Ruskin, 'The Storm-Cloud of the Nineteenth Century,' p. 1339.

25. This terminology of high and low entropy is advanced by Nicholas Georgescu-Roegen in his influential *The Entropy Law and the Economic Process* (Cambridge 1971), which places the question of entropy transformation at the heart of human economic activity.

26. Frederick Soddy, *Matter and Energy* (London 1912), pp. 9–38. Soddy was a pioneer of ecological economics; his range and vigor across a wide variety of disciplines readily call to mind the work of Wells. His most influential texts were *The Interpretation of Radium and the*

Structure of the Atom (1920), 'Cartesian Economics: The Bearing of Physical Science Upon State Stewardship' (1922), and *Money Versus Man* (1935). His construction of knowledge owed a lot more to the physical than to the biological sciences; in 'Cartesian Economics' he makes it clear that he regards 'life' as 'animate mechanism' (London 1922), p. 7.

27. H. G. Wells, *Tono-Bungay* (Lincoln 1978), p. 13. Subsequent citations appear in the text.

28. Susan Stewart, *On Longing: Narrative of the Miniature, the Gigantic, the Souvenir, the Collection* (Baltimore 1984), p. 69.

29. C. F. G. Masterman, *The Condition of England* (London 1909), p. 185. Subsequent citations appear in the text.

30. William Stanley Jevons, *The Coal Question: An Inquiry Concerning the Progress of the Nation and the Probable Exhaustion of Our Coal-Mines* (London 1866), p. 164. For a survey of Jevons's career as an econometrician working to establish economics as 'a mathematical science,' see Margaret Schabas, 'The "Worldly Philosophy" of William Stanley Jevons,' in Patrick Brantlinger, ed., *Energy and Entropy*, pp. 229–47.

31. Erwin Schrodinger makes this point in *What Is Life?* (Cambridge 1967), pp. 72–80. The seed of this idea goes back to Ludwig Boltzmann, who was the first to point out that free energy is the object of the struggle for life. See his 1886 essay, 'Der zweite Hauptsatz der mechanische Warmtheorie,' in *Populare Schriften*, pp. 25–50. Georgescu-Roegen traces this line of affiliation in *The Entropy Law and the Economic Process*, p. 192.

32. See 'The Chapter on Money' in *Grundrisse: Foundations of the Critique of Political Economy* (New York 1973), pp. 115–238.

33. Karl Marx, 'The General Formula for Capital,' *Capital,* Volume I (New York 1977), pp. 247–57.

34. The subtitle of Wells's book directly advertises his sense of the opposition between natural and human history: *The Outline of History: Being a Plain History of Life and Mankind* (New York 1921).

35. Wells particularly explores the open-endedness of the natural world in *The Island of Dr Moreau* (1896).

36. Marx considered incommensurability basic to the act of exchange. His classic text on the morphology of the commodity-form is 'The Fetishism of the Commodity and its Secret,' in *Capital*, Volume I, pp. 163–77.

37. Rudyard Kipling, 'Below the Mill Dam,' in *Traffics and Discoveries* (Harmondsworth 1987), pp. 287–303. The problems of modernizing

mechanics are discussed by L.T.C. Rolt in *Victorian Engineering* (Harmondsworth 1988).

38. Sidney Webb, 'Introduction' to G. W. Goodall, *Advertising: A Study of a Modern Business Power* (London 1914), p. xvii.

39. Jean-François Lyotard advances the thesis that all control is paralogical in character, in *The Postmodern Condition: A Report on Knowledge* (Minneapolis 1984).

40. *The Outline of History*, pp. v–vi.

41. H. G. Wells, 'World Encyclopedia,' in Manfred Kochen, ed., *The Growth of Knowledge: Readings on Organization and Retrieval of Information* (New York 1967), pp. 11, 12.

42. Wells thus performs the work of revising and updating the concept of the world as an enframed totality that Heidegger has seen as basic to modernity; see 'The Age of the World Picture,' in *The Question Concerning Technology and Other Essays* (New York 1977), pp. 115–54.

43. *The Outline of History*, p. 1087.

44. Oswald Spengler, *The Decline of the West*, 2 vols. (New York 1957), Volume I, p. 423.

45. Georges Bataille placed the vitalistic construction of subjectivity at the very center of his project of writing the general economy of the system of human production and consumption. Bataille sees negentropy as the basic condition for the vitalistic overexpenditure of energy, and must be considered the heir of late Victorian visions of the centrality of entropy in the economic process. 'The living organism, in a situation determined by the play of energy on the surface of the globe, ordinarily receives more energy than is necesary for maintaining life; the excess energy (wealth) can be used for the growth of a system (e.g., an organism); if the system can no longer grow, or if the excess can no longer be absorbed in its growth, it must necessarily be lost without profit; it must be spent, willingly or not, gloriously or catastrophically.' *The Accursed Share: An Essay on General Economy, Volume 1, Consumption* (New York 1988), p. 21.

46. James Clerk Maxwell, 'On Governors,' *Proceedings of the Royal Society*, no. 100 (1868), p. 106. Norbert Wiener characterizes Maxwell's article as a foundational text of cybernetics in *Cybernetics: or Control and Communication in the Animal and the Machine* (Cambridge, Mass. 1989), pp. 30–44. He also stresses the governor paradigm in *The Human Use of Human Beings: Cybernetics and Society* (New York 1988; orig. pub. 1954), pp. 136–62.

47. Thomas Pynchon, *Gravity's Rainbow* (New York 1987; orig. pub. 1973), p. 363. Subsequent citations appear in the text.

48. Isaac Newton, *Principia, Volume 1, The Motion of Bodies*, p. 7.
49. *Cybernetics*, p. 132.
50. These connections are anything but arbitrary; a historical logic of sense exists behind each of these fluctuations in the orders of knowledge. When in *Gravity's Rainbow* war becomes cinema and cinema becomes war, Pynchon traces a real dialectic of influence. See Paul Virilio, *War and Cinema: The Logistics of Perception* (London 1989).
51. Claude E. Shannon and Warren Weaver, *The Mathematical Theory of Communication* (Urbana 1949).

CHAPTER FOUR

1. American entrepreneurs like John Holland and Hiram Maxim were notoriously willing to auction off plans to their submarines and guns. They participated in the overall climate of phenomenal disembodiedness we have already seen in the logistics of weapons perception – the readiness to isolate and then detach a line of sight from all other modalities of sense perception. This problematic forms the basis for one of Kipling's best stories, 'The Captive,' dealing with an American inventor peddling newfangled rifles to Boer guerrillas. Deleuze and Guattari see weapons systems as malleable by nature: 'You don't make an atomic bomb with a secret, any more than you make a saber if you are incapable of reproducing it, and of integrating it under different conditions, of transferring it to other assemblages. Propagation and diffusion are fully a part of the line of diffusion.' '1227: Treatise on Nomadology – The War Machine,' *A Thousand Plateaus: Capitalism and Schizophrenia* (Minneapolis 1987), p. 405.
2. In countries like Britain, which faced few internal threats, the nineteenth-century spy system was astonishingly rudimentary. The Foreign Office requires the services of Sherlock Holmes only infrequently, and only then at the behest of his brother Mycroft, a state functionary. In France or Russia, however, it was a different matter, and policing and spy functions shaded into one another (see Conrad's *Under Western Eyes*). This continued during the Cold War, when the Americans separated policing (FBI) and spying (CIA) functions, while the Soviets combined them (KGB).
3. The advent of disinformation signals the breakdown of the circulatory system of the imperial archive. In a 1972 interview, Foucault saw the beginning of the Second World War as the end of the Victorian system of knowledges. 'We can say that the techniques employed up to 1940 relied primarily on the policy of imperialism (the army/the colonies),

whereas those employed since then are closer to a fascist model (police, internal surveillance, confinement). 'On Popular Justice: A Discussion with Maoists,' *Power/Knowledge: Selected Interviews and Other Writings, 1972–1977* (New York 1980), p. 18.

4. The standard history of the British invasion narrative is I.F. Clarke, *Voices Prophesying War, 1763–1984* (London 1966).

5. Quoted in Paul Virilio and Sylvere Lotringer, *Pure War* (New York 1983), p.16.

6. Leo Bersani, 'Pynchon, Paranoia and Literature,' *Representations 25* (Winter 1989), p. 103. For Freud on the etiology of paranoia, see 'Psycho-analytic Notes on an Autobiographical Account of a Case of Paranoia (Dementia Paranoides),' in *The Standard Edition of the Complete Psychological Works of Sigmund Freud*, edited by James Strachey, 24 vols. (London 1953–74), Volume 12, pp. 78–9.

7. The best study of the evolution of logistics is Martin Van Creveld, *Supplying War: Logistics from Wallerstein to Patton* (Cambridge 1977). Clausewitz speaks of the 'friction' of war in *On War*, p. x.

8. For an account of how the postulates of Victorian thermodynamics influenced the development of modern information systems, see James R. Beniger, *The Control Revolution: Technological and Economic Origins of the Information Society* (Cambridge, Mass. 1986), pp. 31–60.

9. Jules Verne, *20,000 Leagues Under the Sea* (New York 1986), p. 126. Further references appear in the text.

10. Once again, Eugenio Donato's view of the museum as failure (he reads the institution through the prism of *Bouvard and Pecuchet*) must be stood on its head. Donato believes that the museum failed to offer 'an adequate continuous representation between Words and Things.' 'The Museum's Furnace: Notes Toward a Contextual Reading of *Bouvard and Pecuchet*,' In Josué V. Harari, ed., *Textual Strategies: Perspectives in Post-Structuralist Criticism* (Ithaca 1979), p. 228. Compare Foucault's account of the successfully interlocking orders of nineteenth-century knowledge in *The Order of Things: An Archaeology of the Human Sciences* (New York 1973), pp. 250–302. See also André Malraux, *Museum Without Walls* (1957), which is less a description of the postwar museum than a nostalgic look backwards at the Victorian museum.

11. In *Speak, Memory* Nabokov describes a person with a modernized version of this interest: filming suicides.

12. Quoted in Virilio, *War and Cinema*, p. 2.

13. This statist teleology pervaded nineteenth-century ethnography and

still informs modern anthropological field work. See Pierre Clastres, *Society Against the State* (New York 1987).

14. Quoted in Paul Virilio, *Speed and Politics*.

15. Quoted in 'Suez Canal,' *Encyclopaedia Britannica*, 1911 edition.

16. Britain waged undeclared wars throughout the nineteenth century; see *Queen Victoria's Little Wars*. Verne's novel, however, introduces a new dynamics of shock into the conduct of undeclared warfare. At the beginning of the century undeclared wars were one-time acts of blow and recoil (as in the Sudan in the 1880s); they then became wars of intermittent shocks (as in South Africa); finally they developed into spaces of continuous phenomenal assault (as in World War I).

17. Verne's novel was a bestseller in England, and with good reason. In *20,000 Leagues* Nemo may well be a paranoid universalization of France's traditional enemy, England. Virilio comments: 'An English cartoon from the nineteenth century shows Bonaparte and Pitt cutting chunks out of an enormous globe-shaped pudding with their sabers, the Frenchman taking the continents while the Englishman claims the sea. This is another way of parceling out the universe: rather than confronting each other on the same terrain, within the limits of the battlefield, the adversaries chose to create a fundamental physical struggle between two types of humanity, one populating the land, the other the oceans.' *Speed and Politics*, p. 37. Like the British, who possessed minimal land forces in 1870, Nemo restricts himself to controlling the sea and exploiting its resources. So thoroughly does Verne, here and in other novels, conform to the geography of the British Empire that many people, today as in the nineteenth century, think of him as a British writer.

18. W. Somerset Maugham, *A Writer's Notebook* (Harmondsworth 1984), p. 21.

19. George C. Thorpe, *Pure Logistics: The Science of War Preparation* (Washington DC 1986), p. 2. Baron Jomini's definition of logistics appears in *The Art of War* (Philadelphia 1873), p. 225.

20. Erskine Childers, *The Riddle of the Sands* (Harmondsworth 1978), p. 101. Further citations appear in the text.

21. Gilles Deleuze and Felix Guattari, *A Thousand Plateaus: Capitalism and Schizophrenia* (Minneapolis 1987), p. 363.

22. This movement toward a collective secret possessed by an entire population can be seen in the case of America's 'stealth' bomber, the secret weapon of the 1990s that has been widely discussed and even photographed.

23. In 'The Myth of the Bridge at the River Kwai' Ian Watt reminds us that the Allies took no action against the bridge the POWs in Thailand built.

Countering the movie, Watt tells a story of international cooperation in protecting the integrity of waterworks. Watt's essay first appeared in 1958; it has since been reprinted in the *Norton Reader*.

24. This emphasis on the rationalization of slowness runs counter to the argument of Paul Virilio's *Speed and Politics*, which sees acceleration as the dominant mode of modern technical control. Silvia Federici and George Caffentzis rightly point out that 'It's not speed that is important, but control. If you can do something quickly, then you can *decide* to do it slowly, if it's in your interest.' They cite the example of electronic banking, where 'it now takes longer to clear checks than before computerization, not because it cannot be done more quickly, but because the higher interest rates make the time the banks hold on to the money more profitable to them.' 'A Review Play on Paul Virilio/ Sylvere Lotringer, *Pure War*,' *Social Text* 17 (Winter–Spring 1987), p. 101.

25. Quoted in Clarke, *Voices Prophesying War*, p. 100.

26. Foucault, 'Two Lectures,' *Power/Knowledge*, p. 81. Foucault refers to the concept of minor knowledges articulated by Deleuze and Guattari in *Kafka: Towards a Minor Literature* (Minneapolis 1986).

27. On the iconography of popular defense, see Paul Virilio, 'Popular Defense and Popular Assault,' in *Autonomia: Post-Political Politics*, *Semiotext(e)*, III, 3 (1980), p. 269.

28. 'Natural hazards, however formidable, are inherently less dangerous and less uncertain than fighting hazards. All conditions are more calculable, all obstacles more surmountable, than those of human resistance. By reasoned calculation they can be overcome almost to timetable. While Napoleon was able to cross the Alps in 1800 "according to plan," the little fort of Bard could interfere so seriously with the movement of his army as to endanger his whole plan.' B. H. Liddell Hart, *Strategy*, p. 163.

29. For a sense of how difficult it is to exercise control over geography, see Bruno Latour, *Science in Action* (Cambridge 1986).

30. Cornelius Ryan brings out the occult character of D-Day in *The Longest Day* (New York 1959), pp. 13–99.

31. Even the ultralinear version of events in B. H. Liddell Hart's *Lawrence of Arabia* (New York 1935) catches the inflection of Lawrence's military mysticism; Hart quotes with approval Lawrence's maxim that 'the perfect general would know everything in heaven and earth' (389).

32. Michel Foucault, *The Archaeology of Knowledge* (New York 1972), p. 129.

33. For an account of the intersecting intelligence bureaucracies of the Second World War, see Christopher Andrew and David Dilks, *The*

Missing Dimension: Governments and Intelligence Communities in the Twentieth Century (London 1984).

34. Thomas Pynchon, *Gravity's Rainbow* (New York 1987), pp. 72–3. Further citations appear in the text.

35. Lord Kelvin, quoted in G. Udny Yule and M. G. Kendall, *An Introduction to the Theory of Statistics*, 12th edition (London 1940), p. 1. Yule and Kendall also explicitly link the theory of statistics with the practice of internal surveillance: 'the progressive modern state finds itself under the necessity of keeping a close and quantitative eye on all that goes on within or without its frontier' (2).

36. Norbert Wiener, *Cybernetics, or Control and Communication in the Animal and the Machine* (Cambridge, Mass. 1948).

37. 'The rockets *are* distributing about London just as Poisson's equation in the textbooks predicts. As the data keep coming in, Roger [Mexico] looks more and more like a prophet. Psi Section people stare after him in the hallways' (54).

38. *Cybernetics*, p. 37.

39. One important continuity exists, however, between the invasion narratives of *The Riddle of the Sands* and *Gravity's Rainbow*: both launch desperate German invasions from island bases in the North Sea, the Frisian Islands (in Childers) and Peenemünde (in Pynchon).

40. 'There is a unity of *composition* of all States, but States have neither the same *development* nor the same *organization*.' *A Thousand Plateaus*, p. 385.

41. K. Marx, *Manuscripts of 1844*, quoted in *A Thousand Plateaus*, p. 460.

INDEX

Printed in the United States
by Baker & Taylor Publisher Services